DATE			

SUPER TANKER!

The Story of the World's Biggest Ships

SUPER

The Story of the

Illustrated with photographs and maps

TEXACO

TANKER!

World's Biggest Ships

GEORGE SULLIVAN

DODD, MEAD & COMPANY/NEW YORK

PICTURE CREDITS

American Institute of Merchant Shipping, 133; American Petroleum Institute, 10 (left), 21, 40, 43, 128; Arabian American Oil Company, 36, 93; The British Petroleum Co., Ltd., 74, 75; Butterworth Systems, Inc., 114 (right); Comsat General Corporation, 79; Consulate General of the Netherlands, 95; Continental Oil Company, 64, 70, 83, 135; C.S.I., 11; Edo Western Corporation, 88, 89; An Esso Photograph, 34; Exxon. 13, 19, 38, 58, 65, 72-73, 76, 77, 81, 87, 108, 114 (left); French Embassy Press & Information Service, 96; Globtik Tankers, Inc., 14; Japanese Information Service, Consulate General of Japan, 39, 55, 57; Joseph Conrad Library, Seamen's Church Institute of New York, 28, 29; Marine Safety International, 67, 69; Mitsubishi Heavy Industries, 31, 48, 54; New York Public Library, 24, 25, 30; New Zealand Consulate General, 18; Nova Scotia Communication & Information Center, 101, 102; Olympic Maritime S.A., 61; Societe Maritime Shell, 8, 12, 91, 92; Sperry Marine Systems, 80; Sun Company, 117; Super Ocean Carrier Conference, 90; Texaco, 23, 33; U.S. Bureau of Mines, 15; U.S. Coast Guard, 105, 107 (Eugene Hoff), 109, 111, 112, 120, 121, 122, 123, 124, 131; U.S. Environmental Protection Agency (Paul Elliot), 110; U.S. Navy, 32. Maps by Dyno Lowenstein, 37, 98, 132. Photographs by George Sullivan, 17, 44, 45, 46, 47, 49, 50, 51, 52, 53, 82, 127.

1 2 3 4 5 6 7 8 9 10

Library of Congress Cataloging in Publication Data

Sullivan, George, 1927-
  Supertanker!

  Includes index.
  SUMMARY: Describes the historical development, design, handling, and problems of the enormous tankers which cruise the seas, carrying oil to a thirsty world.

  1. Tankers—Juvenile literature. [1. Tankers.
2. Ships. 3. Petroleum industry and trade]
I. Title.
VM455.S79   387.2'45   77-16870
ISBN 0-396-07527-4

Acknowledgments

The author is grateful to the many people who helped him in providing source material and photographs that have been used in this book. It would be impossible to name them all, but special thanks are offered the following: Robert Wolk, Joseph Conrad Library of the Seamen's Church Institute of New York; Leo Loftus, Public Affairs Division, and Phil Franklin, U.S. Coast Guard; and Paul Abelson, Seatrain Shipbuilding Corporation.

Contents

The 554,000-ton *Batillus*, the biggest ship in the world, leaves French shipyard at St. Nazaire for sea trials.

1/Energy Lifeline

Picture an oil tanker so big that four football games could be played end-to-end on its deck, and there'd still be room left over for a pair of tennis courts both fore and aft. It's a ship so large that its 41 cargo tanks hold 4 million barrels of oil, enough to keep the United States—all of its cars, homes, and factories—running for six full hours.

Such a ship is no pipe dream. It's the 554,000-ton *Batillus,* at 1,358 feet (414 meters), the biggest ship in the world, an Empire State Building churning through the water.

Built in France, the *Batillus* has been in service since 1976, hauling crude oil from the Persian Gulf, around the Cape of Good Hope, north along the west coast of Africa, then through the Strait of Gibraltar to unload at Fos-sur-Mer, the huge tanker terminal near Marseille that the French have constructed for such seagoing behemoths.

The *Batillus* is not notable merely because of its size. The vessel boasts the latest advances in marine technology. Gyropilot steering enables the ship to keep a preset course without human intervention. A computer bridge system performs all the navigational calculations that used to have to be done manually.

The vessel's anticollision radar system not only reports the presence of nearby ships, but estimates where each is going to be minutes later. "It's almost like having a crystal ball," says one deck officer.

And when the *Batillus* is attempting to snuggle up to a pier, a delicate operation with such an enormous

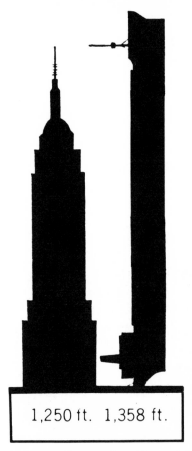

1,250 ft.   1,358 ft.

Left: Enormous propellers and rudders of the *Batillus* dwarf shipyard workers. *Above:* Turned on end, the *Batillus* is more than 100 feet taller than the Empire State Building.

ship, a sonar device helps the pilot maneuver by reporting speed, not in terms of knots—nautical miles per hour—but in the number of feet per minute.

There are so many electronic devices and automatic control systems aboard the *Batillus,* the vessel requires a crew of only 44 men, the same number of men that were required to operate tankers of the 1940s. Yet those ships were less than one-twentieth the size of the *Batillus.*

The *Batillus* is one member of a new generation of ships called supertankers. They represent the most startling advance in marine engineering since that time a century or so ago that sail power gave way to steam.

A tanker's size is measured in deadweight tons (DWT), a term meaning the total tonnage of cargo, fuel, water, and stores the ship can carry. In the years following World War II, when 25,000-ton tankers came into service, people marveled at their size, and sometimes they were even called "supertankers."

By the mid-1950s, tankers of 45,000 tons were being constructed and operated, and before the decade

Engine control room of the *Batillus* is an electronic wonderland.

ended, the 100,000-ton mark was passed. These vessels, too, were often referred to as "supertankers."

But the *real* supertankers—vessels that are 200,000 tons or larger—didn't arrive until the 1960s. Today's supertankers are of two types. The Very Large Crude Carriers (VLCCs) begin at 200,000 tons. The Ultra Large Crude Carriers (ULCCs) begin at 350,000 tons.

Several ULCCs were in service by the early months of 1973. The *Nisseki Maru* (372,400 tons) and the *Globtik Tokyo* (483,650 tons) were launched in Japan. Not only was each, in turn, the biggest ship in the

The *Batillus* under construction at a French shipyard.

Esso Malaysia, at 202,000 tons, is typical VLCC—Very Large Crude Carrier.

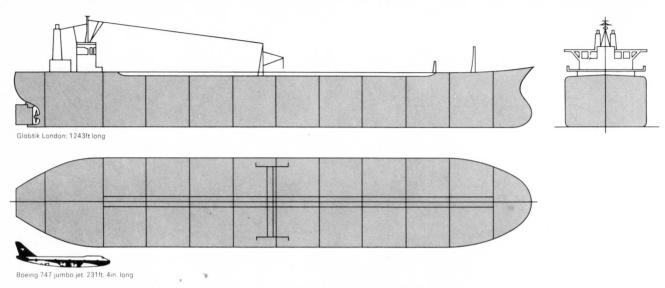

Globtik London: 1243ft long

Boeing 747 jumbo jet: 231ft. 4in. long

Globtik London, 484,000 tons, is classified as a ULCC, an Ultra Large Crude Carrier.

world, but each ranked as the biggest thing man ever put together and expected to move.

The _Batillus'_ billing as the "world's largest" may be only temporary, for a tanker of one million tons is already on the drawing boards. It may become a reality during the 1980s.

The world's tanker fleet consists of approximately 4,500 vessels of more than 6,000 tons. In 1976, 618 of these were supertankers. In terms of numbers, the supertanker fleet represented about 15 percent of the world total. But in terms of total tonnage, supertankers accounted for 46 percent.

Tankers have been important in moving oil supplies to markets around the world since the beginning of the century. But in recent years, insofar as the United States is concerned, tankers have come to be an indispensable energy lifeline.

Oil accounts for about one-half of the energy consumed in the United States. It's expected to remain the

14

Principal tanker routes of the world

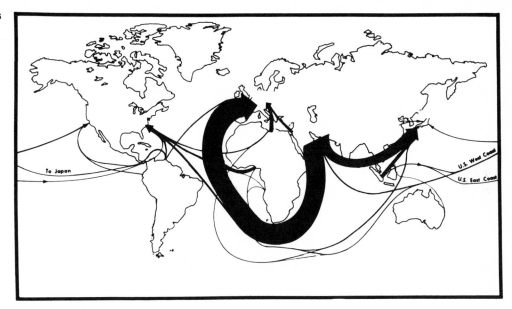

nation's most important energy source for at least another decade or two. While there are many other sources, none is yet regarded as a solution to the energy crisis the nation faces.

The country's coal reserves are abundant, and the use of coal by electric utilities is expected to grow significantly in the years ahead. But coal is not as versatile as oil. Cars cannot burn coal directly. It must first be converted to electricity, coal gas, or synthetic gasoline. Another drawback is that coal is a notorious pollutant.

Gas supplies within the United States are limited. U.S. natural gas production reached a peak in 1972 and has been declining ever since.

The use of nuclear power, like coal, is chiefly connected with the production of electric power. In this regard, nuclear power is likely to rank as the nation's fastest growing energy source in the years ahead, and may eventually replace coal and gas in the production of electric power. But nuclear power plants pose the danger of radiation. Large segments of the population have never been comfortable with them.

Oil shale, a fine-grained rock that is found in enormous quantities in Colorado, Utah, and Wyoming, produces a type of crude oil when crushed and heated. It is an expensive process, however, and creates the problem of what do do with the millions upon millions of tons of shale that are left over. Nevertheless, as conventional oil supplies run out, producers may turn to oil shale.

The future development of hydroelectric power, produced by damming rivers or harnessing waterfalls, is limited because the number of rivers and waterfalls is limited. And the best ones have already been developed.

Geothermal power, which involves tapping hot steam geysers beneath the surface of the earth, has been mentioned as a source of energy. But the number of geysers is limited and they occur in only a few parts of the country. Solar energy, because of the enormous costs involved in gathering and storing it, is practical only in the heating of homes, apartment houses, or office buildings—in space heating. And space heating represents only a small portion of our energy needs. "Solar electric is a long way off," said an official of the Energy Research and Development Administration late in 1976.

Wind-generated electricity has been around for almost a century, but is yet to have an impact on our energy requirements.

What this means is that oil is still king in the United States. And it will be for many years to come.

The United States ranks as one of the leading oil-producing nations of the world. Oil has been found in every state of the union. Louisiana, California, Texas, and Oklahoma have been traditionally ranked as the leading oil-producing states. Huge petroleum reserves were found at Prudhoe Bay in northern Alaska in 1968. Oil from the North Slope began moving through the trans-Alaska pipeline in 1977. Alaska production is expected to reach a peak in the mid-1980s.

The United States now imports more than one-half its oil. Here, in the shadow of the New York skyline, Finnish tanker *Dagny* unloads its cargo at a Bayonne, New Jersey, refinery.

Although the United States produces many billions of barrels of oil each year, our supplies are beginning to dry up. Most experts believe that the United States reached its peak as an oil-producing country in 1970. Since then the nation has had to depend more and more on oil imports. By the mid-1970s, we were importing as much oil as we were producing.

But this oil was being brought to the United States in small-size ships, not supertankers. United States ports are not deep enough to accommodate the big ships. Terminal facilities involving the use of offshore mooring buoys are now in the planning stage, however.

During the 1970s, an energy crisis began to loom for the United States. "No Gasoline" signs appeared at service stations throughout the country in 1973. A natural gas shortage hit during the winter of 1976-1977.

No one has claimed that supertankers are going to be able to solve America's energy problems. But the country thirsts for oil, daily consuming more than 18 million barrels. Many people believe that supertankers can help quench that thirst.

Opposite: Slipway view of *Esso Northumbria,* 254,000 tons, reveals ship's enormous capacity as crude oil carrier.

Natural hot springs are being tapped as an energy source, but their number is limited.

2/Bigger, Bigger, Bigger

One morning late in 1859, a retired railroad conductor, stock market operator, and self-styled "colonel" named Edwin L. Drake was awakened by cries from workers on his drilling rig in Titusville, Pennsylvania. Thick black oil was oozing up from the shaft that had been bored to a depth of 69 feet (21.2 meters). Drake put a pump on the well, and it began producing about 25 barrels a day.

Drake's well is often cited as the beginning of the oil industry in the United States. By the early 1860s, the hills of western Pennsylvania were surging with activity. Wells by the thousands were sunk into the ground. Bustling and crowded oil boomtowns of tents and shanties sprang to life overnight.

By the 1880s, not only Pennsylvania, but Kentucky, Ohio, Illinois, and Indiana were important oil-producing states. In 1901, large-scale production began in Texas with the opening of the Spindletop field near Beaumont, and not long after, Oklahoma began producing oil in important quantities.

The infant industry also developed quickly in foreign countries. Italy began producing oil in 1860, a year after Drake's discovery. Before the turn of the century, production was underway in Canada, Russia, Poland, Japan, Germany, India, Indonesia, Mexico, Argentina, and Trinidad. Significant discoveries of oil were made in the Middle East in 1908.

Today, Colonel Drake is frequently hailed as the "Father of the Oil Industry." Yet the title isn't quite right. There are many things that Drake didn't do.

The world's first commercial oil well. Edwin L. Drake is the man in the top hat and frock coat.

For example, Drake did not discover oil. It had been seeping up from underground springs for centuries. Noah built the ark using pitch, a thick, black, sticky substance derived from oil. Asphalt, another oil product, was used to pave the streets of ancient Babylon. The Greeks routed the Scythian fleet by pouring oil onto seawater and setting it afire. Egyptians used asphalt as axle grease for their chariots.

And long before Drake punched his well into the Pennsylvania soil, men were drilling for oil. The Chinese used bamboo tubes fitted with bronze bits to reach down 3,000 feet for oil in the third century B.C. American Indians used oil for fuel and medicine for hundreds of years before the white man came, and the remains of ancient wells have been found in the oil regions of Pennsylvania, Kentucky, and Ohio.

Oil, usually heavy, dark, and smelly as it comes from the ground, was created from decaying plants and animals that were washed down to the bottom of giant seas that once covered many parts of the earth. As this residue built itself into layers covered with fine sand and mud, it was subjected to tons of pressure from above. This caused the particles to undergo a chemical change, converting them into hydrogen and carbon compounds.

This process, which is still going on, took 40 or 50 million years. To replenish the petroleum that has been consumed since Colonel Drake's day would take another 40 or 50 million years.

The oil derived from Drake's well was refined into kerosene, the chief product of the petroleum industry of the day. Kerosene was used as a fuel in lamps. Ever since colonial times, Americans had been lighting their homes with oil lamps and tallow candles. The kerosene lamp, invented in 1854, was a big step forward.

Refineries of the 1860s also produced gasoline as a by-product of kerosene. But no practical use could be found for it. It exploded when tried in kerosene lamps. Refineries sometimes dumped gasoline into the creeks and rivers to get rid of it.

Pennsylvania crude oil was shipped from the wells to the refineries in wooden barrels that were loaded onto wagons, railroad cars, or river barges. Half-a-million wooden barrels were manufactured in Pennsylvania in 1860. Indeed, there were many more barrelmakers than well-drillers.

Today, oil is shipped by means of pipelines, oil barges, railroad tank cars, and, of course, oceangoing tankers, and rarely by barrel—but the barrel remains the basic unit of measure in the oil industry.

Oil used to be shipped in barrels. This is a scene at a Delaware River terminal in the 1800s.

One barrel is equal to 42 U.S. gallons. It takes, on the average, 7.5 barrels of crude oil to make one long ton. (A long ton, a unit of measurement in the U.S. Customary System, equals 2,240 pounds.)

When the first cargo of oil was shipped across the Atlantic Ocean—from Philadelphia to London—it traveled in barrels. They were carried by the 224-ton *Elizabeth Watts,* a two-masted, square-rigged sailing vessel. The year was 1861.

Liquids had been carried in barrels by ships for many hundreds of years, a practice almost as common as carrying boxed or baled merchandise. The ancient Phoenicians plying the Mediterranean Sea, certainly the Romans, and later the northern European races—the Norsemen, Dutch, and English—transported liquids of many different types in barrels, tubs, and vats.

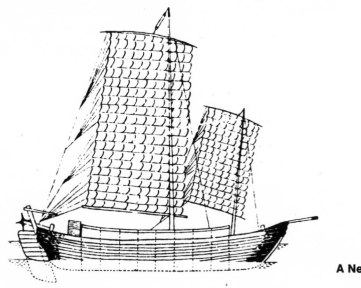

A Newchwang junk

It is no accident that one of the earliest systems of English measurement was based upon the "tun," a large cask for carrying liquids, which was eventually established as the equivalent of 252 gallons. A ship's capacity was measured by the number of tuns it could carry.

Little is known about the voyage of the *Elizabeth Watts*. It could not have been a very pleasant cruise, however. After the ship was finally loaded, a task that took several weeks, the captain was unable to assemble a crew to work on the decks above the foul-smelling oil casks. So he did what any other captain of the day might have done. He ordered that drunken sailors from waterfront bars be sought out and hauled aboard the vessel. By the time the men were regaining their senses, the *Elizabeth Watts* was sailing down the Delaware River, bound for the open sea and England. Despite its rowdy beginning, the voyage was a success.

The barreled shipment of oil between Philadelphia and London became more and more frequent in the years that followed. But this system of transport had obvious disadvantages. An empty barrel itself weighed 64 pounds, and thus a big amount of a vessel's carrying capacity had to be allotted just to barrels.

Oil leaked from the barrels, and the spaces below decks became filled with an evil-smelling vapor. Eventually it seeped into the crew's living quarters. Not only was it unpleasant, it was hazardous, for under the right conditions the gas could explode.

Another drawback was that on the return voyage from England, the vessel could carry no cargo. It had to bring back all those empty barrels.

The solution was to carry the oil in bulk, in one great mass, instead of in individual casks. There were some precedents for this. The Newchwang junks, named for a seaport city in China (now known as Yingkow), were known to have carried oil in bulk during the early 1700s, although they were originally built for carrying water. Once converted to carrying petroleum, these flat-bottomed craft had a capacity of 50 tons.

The Chinese weren't the only ones to carry liquids in ships in bulk. Beginning with the early decades of the nineteenth century, small Italian vessels had brought wine in bulk from ports in southern Italy to ports in the north. Upon arrival, the wine was discharged from the ship's tanks by means of small hand pumps into barrels, crocks, or even pitchers at the dock.

The first iron sailing ship designed to carry crude oil in bulk was constructed in England and launched in 1863. The *Atlantic* was the vessel's name.

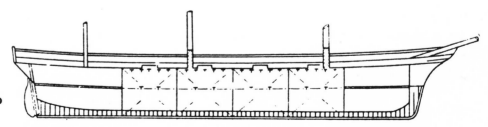

The *Atlantic*, showing cargo tanks.

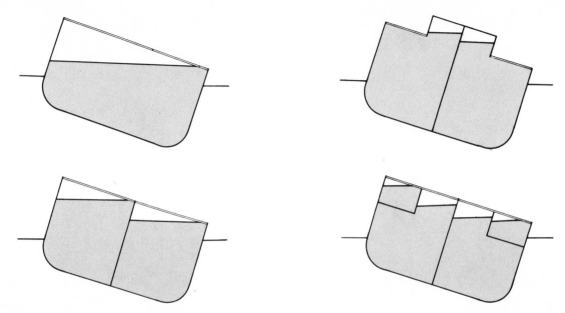

Left: Without partitions in cargo tank (top), oil could roll dangerously from side to side. A center-line partition (bottom) reduced movement. **Right:** An expansion trunk (top) and the construction of smaller tanks in the corners of main tank (bottom) were other methods used to keep oil in check.

In the case of the *Atlantic* and all of the tank ships that were to follow in which the hull itself served as the container for the oil cargo, special design and construction features had to be employed.

One of the greatest dangers to a ship carrying liquid is the effect the movement of the liquid can have upon the vessel's stability. If the ship were to be built so as to provide one, open, undivided tank, the liquid, once set in motion, could slosh about menacingly. Should it begin slamming from side to side, it could even cause the ship to topple over.

The designers of the *Atlantic,* aware of this, used metal partitions to divide the ship's cargo hold into compartments. These partitions served to hold the oil in check.

In time, certain standard methods were developed for subdividing cargo tanks. The simplest was to erect a partition—called a bulkhead—along the center line of the ship, dividing the hold lengthwise into halves. Or the hold might be divided lengthwise into thirds. When the ship rolled, the oil no longer surged in one uncontrolled mass.

Another method was to construct a long and narrow cargo tank that ran the length of the ship and was positioned just above and open to the main compartment. This second compartment was called an expansion trunk. Both the expansion trunk and the main compartment were divided by a common center-line bulkhead.

The main compartment was filled to capacity, then a bit more oil was added. Now, the only oil that could slosh around was the oil that was contained in the expansion trunk, and the amount involved was not big enough to affect the ship's stability.

Still another system was to build side tanks into the top outer corners of the main tank. These smaller tanks extended over the full length of the ship and had the same effect as the expansion trunk, locking the oil in the main compartment firmly in place.

During the nineteenth century, the world of marine engineering went through a period of revolutionary change. A Scottish inventor named James Watt had patented a steam engine in 1769. The invention was soon tried on boats. Robert Fulton, an American, using one of Watt's engines, designed the *Clermont* and saw it launched in 1807. It was the first commercially successful steamboat.

Huge paddle wheels drove the *Clermont* and other steamers. Then in 1836, another inventor, John Ericsson of Sweden, introduced the screw propeller on a commercial vessel. With its several blades mounted on a single hub, the propeller resembled a modern-day electric fan.

The propeller could drive a steamboat with much more efficiency than a paddle wheel. In 1845, the *Great Britain* became the first propeller-driven ship to cross the Atlantic.

Changes in ship design during this period were not limited merely to the engine room. During the late 1700s, British shipbuilders began to construct vessels of iron. Iron ships were cheaper and stronger. And, because wooden ships required extremely heavy timbers, those built of iron were actually lighter in weight. Iron ships began replacing those of wood during the 1800s. Later, iron gave way to steel.

Many of these advances were incorporated in the 2,307-ton *Gluckhauf,* the first tank steamer. Built in England in 1886 for the German-American Petroleum Company, the *Gluckhauf* (the name means "good luck") carried oil in eight big tanks built into the hull.

The ship's engine room was placed in the afterpart of the vessel, an arrangement that made the *Gluckhauf* much easier to handle when empty. The boilers were placed aft of the cargo tanks behind a fireproof wall. The *Gluckhauf* was steam-powered and propeller-driven, but it was also fitted with sails.

While the *Gluckhauf* represented a significant advance, and is often hailed as the prototype of the modern oil tanker, there was no great rush to build tank steamers. Sailing ships continued to play an important role in the transport of oil for years. In fact, oil gave sail a new lease on life. During the 1860s, when electric lighting began to replace the kerosene lamp and the gasoline-powered automobile rolled

The *Gluckhauf,* the first tank steamer.

The *Thomas W. Lawson* was the biggest of the tank sailers.

upon the scene, causing a greater and greater demand for oil, tank sailers of many types—some barrel carriers, others bulk carriers—were pressed into service.

The *Thomas W. Lawson,* built in Quincy, Massachusetts, in 1902, was the largest of the oil sailers. Originally a coal carrier, the vessel was converted to oil transport in 1903, and was used in hauling oil cargo

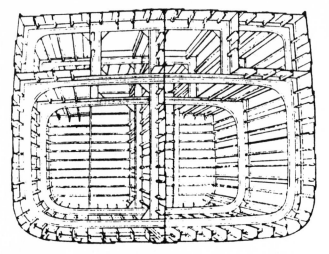

The Isherwood system of framing as applied to a tanker of the early 1900s.

between Texas and Philadelphia for more than ten years. In spite of its size—the vessel was 403 feet in length and had a capacity of 7,800 tons—only 16 men were required to handle the ship.

The Anglo-American Oil Company and the Standard Oil Company both maintained a fleet of fast and efficient tank sailers. Some of these vessels saw active service during World War I. The *Calcutta,* an Anglo-American sailer, carried oil fuel for Navy warships. When peace came in 1918, the *Calcutta* went back into service on the transatlantic run, although it wasn't long before steamer competition forced the ship's retirement.

No book that discusses tank ships would be complete without mentioning Sir Joseph Isherwood, a British ship designer, born in 1870, whose ideas permitted the development of larger tankers. It was usual to use steel beams running the length of the ship to stiffen and strengthen the vessel's hull. Placed at right angles to the beams were a series of frames—or ribs—which held the beams in place. Isherwood devised a method of using stronger frames and placing them at greater intervals. Longer tankers could be built as a result. Even modern supertankers utilize to some extent the construction principles introduced by Isherwood.

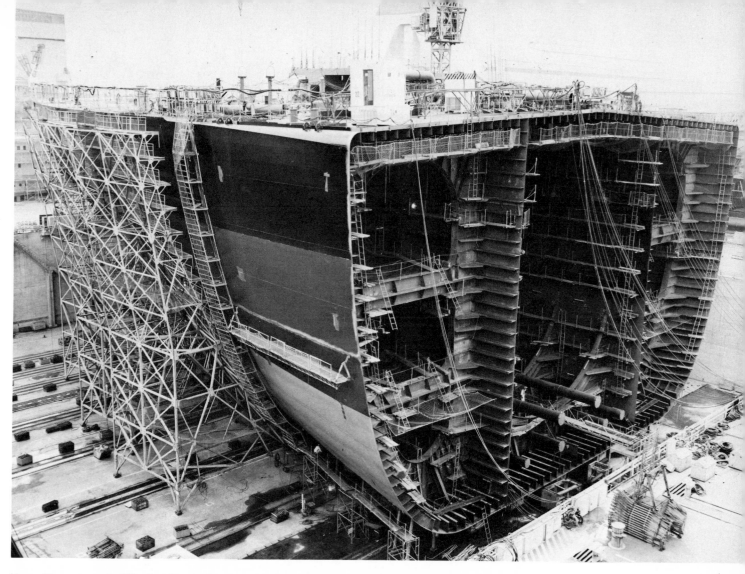

Use of frames and stiffening beams is apparent in this view of a supertanker under construction.

Oil tankers played a crucial role in World War II. The United States exported huge amounts of fuel and lubricants to Russia, France, Great Britain, and the other Allies. Petroleum products, in fact, made up more than one-half of all United States shipments overseas.

Hundreds of World War II tankers were of the T-2 type. The first tanker of this design, the *Esso Gettysburg,* was launched in 1942. T-2 tankers were 523 feet in length and had a deadweight of 16,000 tons. Their 26 tanks carried 141,200 barrels of oil.

These and other tankers of the day followed the lead of standard cargo ships in that they were

A World War II convoy of tankers and cargo ships.

A World War II tanker of the T-2 type. Ships of this design had a deadweight of 16,000 tons.

"three-island" ships. Three structures towered above the main deck like separate islands. At the bow of the ship was a raised deck called the forecastle (pronounced FOLK-suhl). An island at the ship's stern, called the poop, contained living quarters. In between these two structures was the third island, the bridge, from where the ship was navigated and steered. The islands were linked by steel walkways—called catwalks—that were raised several feet above the deck and its clutter of pipes and valves.

After the war ended, the United States began importing more and more oil. Wartime research had helped to spawn the development of hundreds of petrochemicals, chemicals made from crude oil. These chemicals were used in manufacturing synthetic rubber, plastics, paints, medicines, fertilizers, detergents, and a wide array of other products.

At the same time, the nation's consumption of the usual petroleum by-products—gasoline, heating oil, lubricants, and all the others—kept rising.

America's oil shortage began developing during this period, although few people were aware of it. In 1947, for the first time, the United States consumed more oil than it produced.

Bigger tankers were required to meet the spiraling demand for imported oil. In 1948, orders were placed with United States shipyards for the construction of 18 tankers. Two of these were 30,000 tons in size; three were 28,000 tons; and 13 were 26,000 tons. An article in *Business Week* magazine referred to these as "supertankers." But another eighteen years were to go by before the first genuine supertanker would go into service.

In 1954, Stavros Niarchos, who claimed to be the biggest independent tanker operator of the time, took possession of the *World Glory,* at 45,130 tons, the largest tanker ever built. The following year, Daniel K. Ludwig, an American tanker owner and operator, made headlines when he ordered the 84,000-ton *Universe Leader.*

At the time, many nations of the world were depending on the Middle East for oil. Crude from Iran, Iraq, Kuwait, Saudi Arabia, and other Middle Eastern countries was traditionally shipped westward around the Arabian peninsula, north across the Red Sea, and then through the Suez Canal to the Mediterranean Sea. From there, it continued to ports in Europe or the United States.

In 1956, Egypt seized control of the Suez Canal from Great Britain, and closed it down. The move jolted all of western Europe. England was then importing 65 percent of its oil through the Suez passage; France, some 45 percent. The very survival of these and other nations was threatened.

Eventually, the United Nations settled the conflict, and the Canal was reopened. But shipowners and their customers had learned a lesson. They realized that the Suez Canal was like a giant valve, controlling the flow of oil out of the Middle East. That valve could be shut off at any time.

There was an alternative to the Suez passage, however. Tankers from Persian Gulf ports could steam south along Africa's eastern coast, around the Cape of Good Hope, and then north to Europe. But this route stretched the line of supply from 6,500 miles, the distance when using the Suez Canal, to more than

The *Esso Guildford,* 36,000-ton tanker launched in 1957. This is a three-island ship.

An aerial view of Saudi Arabia's Ras Tanura refinery, one of the largest installations of its type in the Middle East.

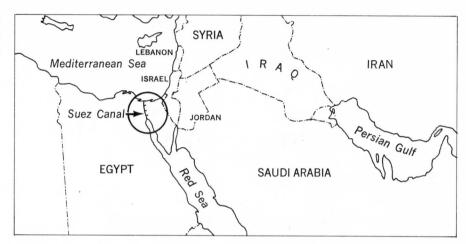

The Suez Canal was once a vital shortcut between Persian Gulf ports and those in Europe.

11,000 miles. Each round trip between the Persian Gulf and Europe was an added 25 days in length.

The longer voyage meant that a tanker made fewer trips to the Persian Gulf over a given period. To maintain the normal flow of Middle Eastern crude to Europe and the United States without depending on the Suez Canal, many more tankers were going to be needed. In fact, the world's tanker tonnage was going to have to be increased by almost 100 percent.

The choice was to build either a tremendous number of small ships, or build big ones and build fewer of them. Economics favored the big ships.

Imagine a box that is 10 feet long, 10 feet wide, and 10 feet tall. Its volume (found by multiplying the outside dimensions of its sides—10 x 10 x 10) is 1,000 cubic feet.

Now double the box's dimensions; it is now 20 feet long, 20 feet wide, and 20 feet in depth. The volume of this box (20 x 20 x 20) is 8,000 cubic feet.

In other words, when you doubled the box's outside dimensions, you didn't merely double the volume of the box, you increased it by 800 percent.

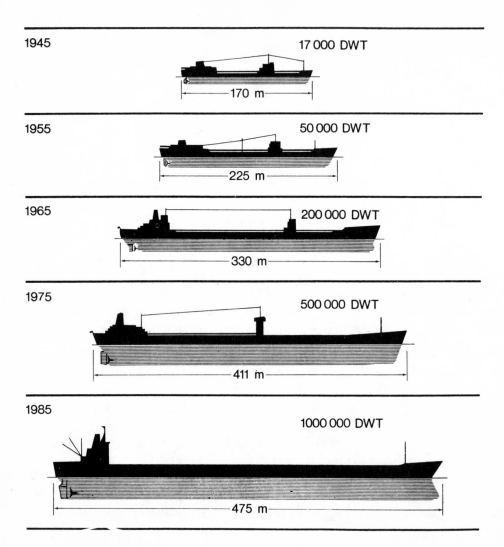

1945   17 000 DWT
170 m

1955   50 000 DWT
225 m

1965   200 000 DWT
330 m

1975   500 000 DWT
411 m

1985   1000 000 DWT
475 m

Comparative tanker sizes

The same thing holds true in the case of a tank—or a tank ship. Double the ship's outside dimensions and you get a vessel several times as big in terms of the amount of oil it can carry.

Another advantage has to do with the efficiency of big vessels. It is one of the principles of hydrodynamics that the larger the vessel, the more easily it slips through the water. Thus, as the size of the tanker increases, the size of the engine to power it has to increase only slightly. A 7,000- to 8,000-horse-

Idemitsu Maru, 210,000 tons, was world's first supertanker.

power engine is required to power a 20,000-ton tanker; but an engine rated at only about 15,000 horsepower is all that is required for a 100,000-ton vessel.

Savings apply to the crew, too. It takes about the same number of men to run a small ship as it does a big one, and sometimes not as many.

Comparing small tankers with very big ones is almost the same as comparing the family automobile with a school bus. Each vehicle requires one engine and one instrument panel. Each requires one driver and set of license plates. The bus uses more gasoline, but not a great deal more. Yet the carrying capacity of the bus, in terms of number of passengers, can be ten or twelve times as great as the automobile's.

Shipbuilders were always aware of the economic advantages inherent in the construction of big ships. The Suez Canal was the reason that they had been reluctant to build them. In order to be able to go through the Canal, a vessel could draw no more than 35 feet (10.7 meters), the draft of a 38,000-ton tanker. Thus, with only a handful of exceptions, the world's tanker fleet was made up of vessels that were no bigger than 38,000 tons.

But with the closing of the Suez Canal in 1956, the barrier it presented was removed. Shipbuilders throughout the world scrambled to build bigger and bigger tankers.

In 1957, the world's largest tanker was 56,000 tons.

In 1959, the largest tanker was 114,000 tons.

In 1962, the largest tanker was 130,000 tons.

In 1966, the first supertanker, the 210,000-ton *Idemitsu Maru,* was launched in Japan.

By the following year, six 312,000-ton tankers were under construction, and designs for 400,000-ton and 500,000-ton vessels were in preparation. The age of the supertanker was at hand.

Globtik Tokyo, **483,000 tons, ranked as the world's largest ship—but not for very long.**

3/From Steel Plate

Cutting torches crackle. Crane engines hum. Warning bells clang. Thick steel plates creak and groan as they are cut and bent into intricate shapes. Out of this bedlam at a converted Navy shipyard on the shore of the East River in Brooklyn, New York, the T.T. (for Turbo Tanker) *Bay Ridge* is taking shape.

The T.T. *Bay Ridge* is the fourth in a series of supertankers being built by the Seatrain Shipbuilding Corporation at the Brooklyn site. They are among the biggest ships ever built in the United States, and the biggest ever to fly the American flag.

The T.T. *Bay Ridge,* like its three sister ships, will be 225,000 deadweight tons. The vessel is 1,094 feet (334 meters) in length; its breadth is 143 feet (44 meters). Fully loaded, the ship has a draft of 70 feet (22 meters). The cargo tanks of the T.T. *Bay Ridge* are capable of carrying 1½ million barrels of crude, enough to fill a 50-mile line of tanker trucks, or to power the automobiles and heat the homes of such cities as Green Bay, Wisconsin, or Bethlehem, Pennsylvania, for an entire winter.

Ships used to be constructed on inclined slipways. The keel, the backbone of the ship, extending fore and aft on the center line, would be laid flat on the slipway. Then the steel ribs that were to form the hull skeleton—called frames—would be welded to the keel. Next, steel plates were welded across the frames, so as to form the hull. When the ship was completed, it was launched, that is, permitted to slide down the slipway into the water.

Guided by tugs, T.T. *Brooklyn* eases toward the sea for operating trials.

With supertankers, it's usually much different. The ship is put together in a dry dock, a structure that resembles a huge concrete bathtub, the bottom of which is well below water level. Powerful cranes hoist completed ship sections into the dry dock, and one by one they are fitted into place. When the vessel's hull is completed, the dry dock is flooded like the lock of a canal and the ship floats.

For a vessel such as the T.T. *Bay Ridge,* which is about a fifth of a mile long, a dry dock at least that long is required. Several such dry docks are available at the Seatrain site in Brooklyn, a shipyard with a rich history.

It was founded as the Brooklyn Navy Yard in 1801. More than a hundred vessels were fitted out there for the War of 1812. The yard also played an important role in the Civil War and the Spanish-American War, serving as a focal point for Navy construction and supply. During World War I, shipyard activity expanded, reaching a peak during World War II when more than 60,000 workers turned out huge aircraft carriers, battleships, and other vessels for the U.S. fleet.

The Navy closed the shipyard in the late 1960s. About one-half of the yard was taken over by the Seatrain Corporation in January, 1969. Besides the T.T. *Bay Ridge,* the other supertankers constructed there were the T.T. *Brooklyn,* T.T. *Williamsburg,* and T.T. *Stuyvesant.*

Several hundred men work on each ship. They include welders and cutters, carpenters and electricians, and pipefitters and machinists.

Construction begins when barges bring railroad flatcars carrying plates of raw steel to the shipyard's

A tall stack of steel plate, the basic ingredient in tanker construction.

unloading piers. The plates are lifted from the flatcars by the electromagnets of a big overhead crane, and stacked in tall piles.

In the first stage of construction, the plates move one by one along a conveyer line into the preparation shop, a building as long as three football fields. Here a machine blasts each plate with a steady stream of metal shot, thoroughly "scrubbing" its flat surfaces. Then the plates are spray-painted with a special epoxy coating that serves as a protective skin.

Years ago, men with wooden patterns and steel measures would laboriously chalk lines on the steel plates to be used as guides in cutting them into the proper shapes. Then other men with acetylene torches would do the cutting. Those days have gone the way of tank sailers. In modern shipyards like the one in Brooklyn, electric eyes following 1-to-100 scale patterns automatically guide torch cutters over unchalked plates.

The plates move on another conveyer line onto what is known as the flat-panel line. Here the plates will be welded together to form decks, bulkheads, and outer or bottom hull sections.

A crane lifts the cut panels one by one from the conveyer line, and deposits each in a preassigned location on a bed of upright short steel posts. When all the panels are in place on this fitting bed, welding begins.

In welding, heat is applied along the adjoining edges of two steel sections, and metal with a low melting point is used to fill the seam. Ships used to be riveted together. Welding didn't become commonplace until World War II, when there was a great demand for ships. Many people looked upon the first welded ships with suspicion, saying they were not practical as oceangoing vessels. There was some evidence to support this idea, for more than a few of the early welded ships cracked or split apart. Sound welding techniques took years to develop.

Welding is all done automatically today. There are about a dozen different types of automatic welders. Some weld horizontally; others weld vertically. Still others are capable of welding in a circular pattern, as when two pipe sections are being joined.

Plates are welded together to form decks, bulkheads, and hull sections.

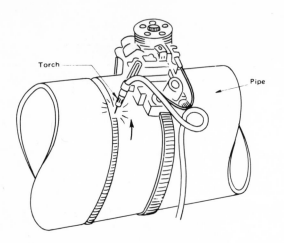

Torch

Pipe

**Some automatic welders move
in a circular pattern.**

When the steel panels are welded on one side, a bridge crane flips over each section. The section is then welded on the other side. Sections weighing as much as 200 tons can be handled in this manner.

Once a section is completed, the crane carries it to the extreme end of the flat-panel building where L-shaped or T-shaped beams are welded to it. These stiffen and strengthen the section.

Alongside the flat-panel building is a similar shop where curved panels are fabricated. It is equipped with huge presses, and bending and cutting machines. One frame bender uses a force of up to 700 tons in producing curved shapes the ship requires.

When finished, the flat sections and the curved sections are lifted from their conveyer lines by a transporter, a big rubber-tired vehicle that looks like a flatbed truck without the cab. It has 48 wheels on twelve axles. It moves under a completed section, lifts it up, and hauls it to the painting shop. Each of the sections is spray-painted several times.

After completed sections have been painted, they are hauled by the transporter to the dry dock. Enormous whirley cranes hoist each section into place. Little by little the ship begins to take shape.

One of the most difficult jobs is getting the propeller shaft positioned in a perfectly straight line. If the shaft were to be out of alignment by as much as one-thousandth of an inch, serious problems could result.

As sections are fitted together in the dry dock, ship begins to take form. *Right:* Stern section of T.T. *Bay Ridge* awaits mounting of propeller.

Six-bladed propeller of T.T. *Stuyvesant*, cast from copper, nickel, aluminum, and bronze, weighs 67 tons, has diameter of 27½ feet. But it looks small next to ship's towering rudder.

In days past, a tightly strung steel wire or a surveyor's transit was used in aligning the shaft. But at the Seatrain shipyard, a laser beam is used. In attempting to produce a perfectly straight line, no other method is as precise as the laser's focused rays of light. A laser beam is also used in aligning the rudder shaft.

After the hull and much of the superstructure have been completed, and the engines and the boilers are in place, the ship is ready to be moved to the nearby outfitting pier. Workers open valves and flood the dock. The ship gently floats off the blocks on the bottom of the dry dock that have been supporting its weight. When the water level inside the dock reaches the level of the water outside, the huge dock doors—called caissons—are swung open.

Just before the vessel is towed out of the dock, it is christened. A woman is chosen to act as the ship's sponsor. She names the vessel as she breaks a bottle of champagne over its bow.

There is still a good deal more work to be done on the ship. After tugs have nudged the vessel to its outfitting pier, its boilers and engines are tested. The anchors and anchor chains are hoisted aboard. The lifeboats and other safety equipment are added. Electrical wiring and fixtures are added. Deck piping is laid down.

At outfitting pier, T.T. *Stuyvesant* is tended by whirley cranes.

Anchor chain for T.T. *Stuyvesant* is soon to be hoisted aboard.

Opening in hull's side shows placement of ship's turbines.

After several months at the outfitting pier, the ship is ready for three or four days of trial runs. It is manned by a crew of about one hundred men, most of whom are shipyard workers. Others represent the company that is to own the ship. Since the number of workers on board is more than three times the number of people who will eventually man the ship, conditions are crowded. Cots are set up in the deckhouse; meals are served in several sittings. "It's hardly a pleasure cruise," says one worker.

Operating under its own power, the ship heads out into the open sea. There it is made to perform various speed and maneuvering trials. The propulsion machinery is thoroughly tested and fuel consumption is measured at various speeds. Every piece of equipment is tried out. At the end of the trials, the ship heads back to the yard. Workmen then make whatever adjustments are necessary.

A second trial run follows. But this time it is more of a training session for men who are going to serve as the ship's crew. Shipyard workers instruct them in the operation of the vessel and all of its equipment.

During 1976, contracts were signed for the construction of a pair of Ultra Large Crude Carriers, each to be 390,000 deadweight tons, at the Newport News Shipbuilding Company in Newport News, Virginia. Work on the two vessels began late in 1977. They were scheduled for completion during the 1980s.

Despite this activity, the United States is not one of the leading nations in supertanker construction. Japan, France, Spain, England, West Germany, Sweden, Norway, and the Netherlands are among the nations that surpass the United States.

Japan is the world leader. In the midst of the tanker-building boom of the late 1960s and early 1970s, more than half of all supertankers were built in Japan.

Japan's Nagasaki shipyard is one of the world's largest.

Many modern shipbuilding methods were developed in Japanese yards. This is a scene at the Nagasaki shipyard of Mitsubishi Heavy Industries.

The reasons for Japan's supremacy in supertanker construction evolved out of World War II. Toward the end of the war, the Japanese merchant marine and navy began to experience heavy losses. In their desperation to replace their destroyed and sunken ships, the Japanese built shipyards almost everywhere a port was located. They also developed new and speedy construction techniques.

Japanese shipyards escaped serious damage during the war. The sprawling navy yard at Kure was left intact by Allied bombers, and the huge dry dock there, which was capable of accommodating 150,000-ton ships, was ready to serve in a shipbuilding role as soon as the war ended. Even in Nagasaki, the target for the second atomic bomb, the huge Mitsubishi shipyard was scarcely damaged. Tens of millions of dollars were spent in expanding operations in Nagasaki after the war, and today it is the site of the biggest shipyard in Japan.

Japan's wish to establish itself as the No. 1 shipbuilding nation of the world was not based solely on the expectation of profits to be made. It was somewhat of a necessity. Japan has to import practically all of its raw materials. Ships by the hundreds were needed after World War II. The Japanese were quick to realize that iron ore and crude oil could be carried more cheaply in ships of super size.

Many advanced construction techniques are used by Japanese shipbuilders. One is "jumbo-izing," which serves to boost the cargo-carrying space of an existing tanker. First, the tanker is cut in two, and then a new mid-body section is welded in between the two ends. Using this technique, the *Olympic Runner,* a 40,471-ton vessel, was stepped up in size to 59,000 tons. The *Olympic Rider* weathered similar surgery.

The Japanese also are capable of welding hull sections together in the water. For example, two 200,000-ton ship sections would be built in separate dry docks, floated, then joined to form a 400,000-ton vessel.

The rush to expand supertanker fleets, detailed in a previous chapter, had to end. And it did, very abruptly.

At Japan's Negishi shipyard, one-half of a supertanker is nudged by tugs toward the other half, waiting in its graving dock. They'll be welded together.

Late in 1973, Iran, Saudi Arabia, Kuwait, and the other members of the Organization of Petroleum Exporting Countries boosted the price of crude oil dramatically. The cost of a barrel of crude went from $2.85 to $10.

At the same time, the United States and many other countries began experiencing a period of economic recession.

Oil purchases dipped as a result. When they did, the demand for new tankers came to a standstill.

The future is uncertain. As far as the United States is concerned, help may come in the form of a cargo preference law, which the federal government has considered enacting. Such a law would require that a certain percentage of the crude oil we import be brought to United States ports in American-built flagships.

Both houses of Congress passed a cargo preference bill in 1974. But it was vetoed by President Gerald Ford.

Those opposed to a cargo preference law claim that it would add to the cost of imported oil. Nevertheless, were such legislation to become a reality, it should surely trigger a shipbuilding boom. The activity that now surrounds the T.T. *Bay Ridge* as it takes form in a Brooklyn dry dock might be duplicated in other shipyards on both coasts and the Gulf of Mexico.

Despite the lull in shipbuilding activity, recent years have seen a number of innovations in supertanker construction. The *Aiko Maru,* a 406,000-ton vessel that went into service in 1976, is a case in point. Despite the *Aiko Maru's* enormous size, its draft is about the same as that of a 200,000-ton ship.

In building the *Aiko Maru,* Japan's Mitsubishi company was able to get increased size without increasing the draft by simply building the vessel wider. The *Aiko Maru* is, in fact, the widest ship in the world, wider even than the *Batillus,* 230 feet vs. 200 feet (70 meters vs. 63 meters).

A wide hull normally works to cut a vessel's speed and restrict its maneuverability. But not as far as the

Esso Gascogne, **256,000 tons, nears completion in a Birmingham, England, shipyard.**

Aiko Maru is concerned. A special hull design, developed after repeated experiments, helps the ship overcome the usual problems of wideness. For one thing, the ship's bow is not rounded, but vertical. It cuts through the water like a knife.

Supertankers of the future are not all going to be notable merely for their dimensions or how much oil they can carry. *What* they carry may make them unique. In some cases, it may be something else besides crude oil.

Many countries of the Middle East have announced plans to build huge oil refineries. Construction is already underway at some sites. The output of these refineries will be so great that it will exceed the demands of Middle Eastern markets. Thus, the newly refined products—gasoline, kerosene, or fuel oil—will have to be shipped to the present crude markets, to western Europe, Japan, and the United States.

Instead of building a new fleet of tankers for this purpose, it's been suggested that present-day supertankers be converted so as to be able to handle these products, while at the same time still be able to carry crude. For example, a typical 250,000-ton supertanker might be converted to handle 50,000 tons of fuel oil, say, plus 20,000 tons of crude. Besides redesigning some of the vessels' tanks, a separate pumping system for the fuel oil would have to be installed.

All supertankers of the world might one day be completely overshadowed by a vessel that was proposed not long ago—a tanker of one million tons. Andrew G. Spyrou, Technical Director of the A. S. Onassis Group of Companies, says that he is "optimistic" that such a ship will be a reality one day.

The million-ton tanker might be powered by nuclear energy. A nuclear reactor would serve as the source of heat, similar to the furnace of a boiler. The heat could be released at any desired rate or temperature.

Using nuclear power to drive a ship through the water is not something new. The first nuclear-powered ship, the submarine *Nautilus,* was launched in 1954. A nuclear merchant ship, the *Savannah,* began operation in 1959, but was retired in 1971. The Navy, besides its atomic-powered submarine fleet, operates several other nuclear vessels, including a number of huge aircraft carriers.

A one million-ton tanker would have a draft of over 100 feet, and thus would be excluded from many of the world's tanker routes. Loading in the Persian Gulf would be no problem, however. The water is deep

An artist's conception of a one million-ton supertanker.

enough there, and adequate terminal facilities have been developed. Once loaded, the vessel could steam south and round the Cape of Good Hope without difficulty.

But when it came to delivering the crude, it could encounter some problems. The huge vessel would have to steer clear of Rotterdam and Le Havre, nor is the Dover Strait deep enough to permit the safe passage of a tanker drawing 100 feet.

There are two solutions. The million-ton vessel could put in at Bantry Bay in southern Ireland, and then pump its oil into smaller tankers. Transshipment facilities are already in operation there. Or the ship could enter the Mediterranean Sea through the Strait of Gibraltar, and feed Europe from the south, from Fos-sur-Mer in France or Genoa in Italy.

The usual route to Japan would be closed to a one million-ton tanker. The Strait of Malacca between the Malayan Peninsula and Sumatra is not deep enough. Instead, the ship would have to steam across the Indian Ocean until it reached the Lombok Strait, off Java's eastern tip, head north through the Strait, then into the South China Sea and Japan.

Inspecting the tanks of a one million-ton ship would be an enormous task. The total vertical distance involved would be equivalent to climbing Mount Everest, the highest peak in the world, and there'd still be another mile to go.

Steel plates below the waterline would be inspected while the vessel was loading or unloading—but human eyes would not do the job. Instead, every square inch of the hull would be photographed by an underwater motion picture camera, the camera crew working alongside the ship from a small boat. The film produced would be screened frame by frame.

The million-ton ship would never stop moving, except for those brief intervals necessary to take on crude or pump it off. And every four or five years, the vessel would have to enter a dry dock for a thorough inspection. But otherwise it would be perpetually on the move, a restless giant steaming the oceans of the world.

4/Satellites and Sextants

From a distance, the low silhouette of a fully laden supertanker makes it difficult to appreciate the vessel's enormous size. Nor are there very many clues to the sophisticated technology that's used in operating the ship.

But pay a call on a supertanker that's moored to a harbor buoy, and you quickly become aware of the ship's true nature. As your boat pulls alongside the ship, you feel dwarfed by the long wall of steel that rises up before you, blocking all else from view.

And when you go aboard and visit the bridge to see the array of buttons, switches, and cathode ray tubes that command computers and, in some cases, enable deck officers to communicate with satellites, you know immediately that this is no ordinary vessel.

A computer steers the vessel along its route, continuously monitoring the movement of the rudder. In approaching crowded harbors, an unusual radar system tells which ships to avoid and how to avoid them. A computer supervises the loading and unloading of the ship's cargo. In the engine room, computers monitor basic temperatures, pressures, and flow rates.

The ship seems to be able to run itself. One observer, in fact, has forecast the day that such vessels will be managed by a small team of technician-navigators, no larger than the flight crew of an airliner. Even the day of unmanned ships, sailing the seas by remote control, has been predicted.

From the bridge, supertanker looks like this.

But Captain Arrigo Pierallini, a VLCC master—or captain—since the first days these ships began to sail, glowers at this suggestion. "Sure, all these electronic systems are great," he says. "But they can only do so much." Captain Pierallini puts a finger to his head. "There's no substitute for the brain," he says.

In his more than two decades of experience with the Exxon Corporation's tanker fleet, Captain Pierallini, a smallish man with thinning black hair and flashing dark eyes, has been given increasingly responsible commands. He takes pride in having served as the master of some of the biggest ships ever built.

"Suppose we're in the English Channel," he says, "and far ahead there's a fishing trawler that looks like it's trying to cross our bow. Do we have the right of way—or does the trawler?

"In other words, there's a decision to be made, and shipboard computers don't make such decisions. It comes down to human judgment."

To Captain Pierallini, VLCCs don't present any special operating problems. "It's simply a matter of 'more,' " he says. "For stopping or turning, or whatever else you plan to do, you need *more* room and *more* time. You need *more* water.

"Once you get used to that concept, it's almost like sailing any other ship."

Captain Pierallini's confidence may stem, at least in part, from all the special training he's received. It includes a two-week course in supertanker handling given at a training center located near Grenoble, France. There prospective tanker captains maneuver models about an oval nine-acre lake that was built by the Trappist monks in the seventeenth century to provide fish for the tables of French monarchs.

At training center near Grenoble, France, supertanker model moves through a replica of a channel in the Suez Canal.

The largest of the models, the *Antifer,* is a 1-to-25 scale copy of the 400,000-ton *Esso Japan.* The model holds three men.

From a distance, the model bears a fairly close resemblance to the life-size tanker, but close inspection reveals it has none of the fittings of a real ship—no pipes, walkways, or ladders, as are found on the deck of a real tanker. The model's deck is broken so as to provide a seating area for the trainees.

But the model performs exactly as a real tanker does, with an electric motor producing the same equivalent power as the engines of the big ship. There's also an equivalent time lag when the captain seeks to increase or decrease speed, and the movement of the model's rudder corresponds with that of the real tanker.

The captain sits with his eyes at the same relative level they would be if he were standing on the bridge of a full-sized ship. If the bow of his model blocks the view of a buoy or the shoreline, he knows that the big ship will obscure his vision in the same manner. Each model is equipped with a radio that permits conversations with captains in other models, and with the instructors, who supervise the exercise from conventional powerboats.

There is no pleasure cruising. "You can't relax for a minute," says one captain. "You have to concentrate all the way."

The lake has been carefully shaped to form shoals, bays, channels, and deepwater area, all in the same 1:25 scale. It also offers a 400-foot-long replica of an actual bend in the Suez Canal.

Scale models of three mooring buoys, arranged in a semicircle and held stationary by anchors, are used in practicing mooring. To tie up at the buoys, the captain brings his ship into position and drops both anchors. He then reverses his engine, backing the model toward the buoys, paying out anchor chain as it moves. When the ship is close enough, mooring wires are carried from the ship's stern to the buoys. These, along with the anchors, hold the ship in a fixed position.

A floating pier, held by one anchor to permit it to swing into the wind, is used in teaching captains the principle of ship-to-ship berthing. Frequently a supertanker must pump a portion of its cargo to a smaller vessel. This reduces the draft of the larger ship, permitting it to enter a relatively shallow harbor.

Another model pier, this one stationary, is used in training captains to dock. This pier is fitted out with

This is training by simulator. Harbor scene is produced on huge curved screen. Trainee mans wheelhouse controls.

four sensitive bumpers that measure the model's impact as it comes alongside. These work in combination with traffic lights which stand at each of the pier ends. If the docking is a good one, no lights flash. If his ship gives the dock a gentle nudge, a green light flashes. A heavy jolt causes a yellow light to flash. Should the model slam hard into the pier, a red light flashes and a loud klaxon squawks, meaning that if it had been a real-life situation, the impact would have demolished the dock.

Tanker officers are also trained by simulator. In simulation training, computers create both routine and emergency tanker operating conditions within a wheelhouse arranged just like an actual wheelhouse aboard ship. The trainees respond by working actual controls. "With the simulator, we can give a tanker officer the equivalent of several months' shipboard experience in four or five days," says Albert J. Uletschi, president of Marine Safety International, whose firm began operating one of the most sophisticated of such simulators at the Marine Air Terminal at New York's LaGuardia Airport in 1977.

A captain can be taught, for example, how to handle and maneuver a supertanker when entering the harbor of Milford Haven, Wales, one of the world's few good deepwater ports. From inside the wheelhouse, the trainees observe the ship's progress from live television images projected on an enormous curved screen that fills the entire viewing area through the bridge windows.

Buoys and beacons flash. Buildings, oil storage tanks, and berths seem to sweep by on each side. Degrees of fog, wind, and current can be simulated. "The only difference between this and Milford Haven," said one captain, "is that in Milford Haven it's generally raining."

The operation is directed by an instructor sitting at a control panel at the rear of the wheelhouse. He can take the trainees through a routine approach to a berth, or simulate an emergency—a rudder or engine failure, or a breakdown in radio or navigation equipment. The instructor is able to monitor how the trainee reacts to each exercise.

A wrong move by a trainee at the ship's controls that results in a grounding causes no hull damage or oil spill—only an electronic "beep." And then the ship comes to an abrupt stop.

The heart of the simulator is a television system with a three-camera, wide-angle optical probe that scans the face of a wall-sized model board of the Milford Haven harbor. The board, prepared on a 2,000-to-1 scale, has all the topographical features of the real harbor, including ships, piers, islands, and lighthouses. Handcrafted from thousands of photographs and charts, the model represents a 50-square-mile area.

As the probe, responding to signals from the "bridge," moves across the face of the board, video signals are transmitted to projectors below the "wheelhouse." These produce life-sized images onto the curved screen.

To change the "program," it's simply a matter of rolling another board before the optical probe. Besides Milford Haven, Marine Safety International has several other reproductions available, including one for Ras Tanura, the big tanker terminal in Saudi Arabia. Two other such simulator training schools have been in operation in Holland for several years.

Besides being trained under simulated conditions, tanker officers attend schools for instruction in shiphandling and the use of navigation radar, in fire fighting and pollution prevention. There's also a personnel safety course to prepare officers for medical emergencies. Officers may also travel as trainees

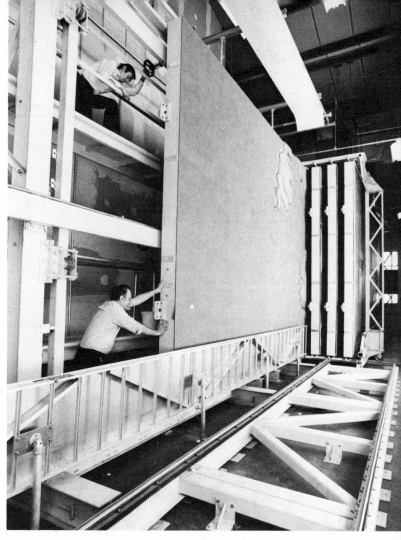

Left: Close-up of television camera as it moves over the face of a model board that represents Milford Haven harbor.
Right: To transmit a new "program," it's simply a matter of sliding another model board into place.

Seamen test fire nozzles during drill aboard *Conoco America*.

aboard the vessel on which they are later to serve, in order to learn the behavior of the ship under different operating conditions.

Aboard the typical 200,000- to 300,000-ton tanker, the master commands approximately 10 officers and 20 crew members. The deck officers, who navigate the ship and oversee the work of the deck crew, report directly to the captain. They're called mates. There's a first mate, second mate, and third mate. The first mate is usually the ship's navigator.

Officers aboard U.S. merchant ships have often received their training at the U.S. Merchant Marine Academy at Kings Point, New York, which is equal in status to the academies of the U.S. armed forces. In addition to the Merchant Marine Academy at Kings Point, five states have maritime academies.

After graduation, an officer must serve an apprenticeship of 18 months to two years aboard a ship before being eligible to take a junior license examination. Additional years of experience and several other examinations are required before a junior officer can hope to become a master or chief engineer.

The deck crew is made up of both able-bodied seamen and ordinary seamen. Able-bodied seamen have the greater amount of experience, and are assigned the more responsible tasks—making shipboard repairs, standing lookout watches, and serving as helmsmen, that is, each man qualified takes his turn at the wheel.

The ordinary seamen keep the ship clean and do the maintenance work. Painting the ship and then immediately repainting it used to be among the principal duties that a deckhand performed, but a supertanker gets a virtually indestructible vinyl coating instead of paint. There's hardly ever any need to paint.

The chief officer and the pumpman are responsible for the loading and discharging of the cargo, and the maintenance of the cargo tanks. In days past, this meant descending by means of a spindly ladder into the dark and smelly tanks after the ship had been unloaded, and scooping up the sludge and rust that had been left behind.

Because of the lethal vapors in the tanks, each man had to wear a special breathing apparatus. Some men feared the job of inspecting the tanks; others merely hated it.

Automatic washing systems (discussed in a later chapter), since they are more efficient in their cleansing action, have about eliminated the need for tank inspections. If, however, a monitoring device should

Cross Section of a Very Large Crude Carrier

LENGTH: 1,141 feet
BEAM: 170 feet
DEADWEIGHT: 253,000 tons
SPEED: 16 knots

1. CHOCK
2. VENTS
3. MOORING WINCH
4. CHOCK
5. RUDDER SHAFT
6. RUDDER
7. MOORING BITTS
8. PROPELLER
9. LADDER
10. SWIMMING POOL
11. STERN LIGHT
12. HOIST
13. ENGINE ROOM (UPPER LEVEL)
14. BOILER
15. AUXILIARY GENERATORS
16. PROPELLER SHAFT

17. PROPELLER SHAFT BEARING
18. GEAR CASE
19. HIGH AND LOW PRESSURE TURBINES
20. CONDENSER
21. MAIN BOILER
22. WATER OVERBOARD DISCHARGE
23. DIESEL GENERATOR
24. UPTAKE FUNNEL
25. SETTLING TANKS
26. BALLAST TANKS
27. PUMP ROOM
28. LIFEBOAT CRANE
29. BRIDGE WING
30. RADAR AND SIGNAL MAST
31. WHEELHOUSE
32. PUMP ROOM VENT
   a WALKWAY
   b RAMP
   c BREAKWATER
33. SEPARATOR
34. BULKHEAD
35. STABILIZATION OPENINGS IN BULKHEADS
36. CARGO LINES TO PUMP ROOM
37. CENTER KEEL

38. BULKHEAD
39. FRAMES
40. TANK BRACKETS
41. WALKWAY
42. ELECTRICAL CABLE TRAY
43. FOAM SPRAYERS
44. DECK LIGHTS
45. REINFORCING FRAME
46. WING TANK WEB FRAME
47. DECK GIRDER
48. BULKHEAD FRAMES
49. OPERATING PANEL FOR HOSE DERRICKS
50. HOSE DERRICK AND MAST
51. LADDER
52. LADDER HOIST
53. CENTER DECK GIRDER
54. CARGO TANK LADDERS
55. SIDE KEEL
56. OPENING FOR TANK WASHERS
57. HOSE SUPPORT
58. GUARD FOR HYDRAULIC LINES
59. HOSE TROUGH
60. TANK WASHING MACHINE
61. WALKWAY

62. TANK HATCH
63. CHOCK
64. FRAMES
65. WASH BULKHEAD
66. SIDE FRAMES
67. CENTER TANK
68. FOREMAST
69. ANCHOR WINDLASSES
70. COMPANIONWAY
71. HATCH
72. TANK VENT
73. ANCHOR-CHAIN ROLLER
74. FOREPEAK BULKHEAD
75. FOREPEAK
76. WARNING LIGHT
77. ANCHOR LIGHT
78. WATERLINE

report that there is something wrong with a tank—a valve may be malfunctioning, for instance—crewmen will be sent in for a look. Otherwise, the tanks are kept sealed.

The engine room operation is headed by the chief engineer. Helping him are the first, second, and third assistant engineers. Like the captain and the deck officers, each of the engineering officers must be licensed.

The engines of most big tankers are steam turbines. Steam from the ship's boiler spins the turbine's bladed wheel in somewhat the same way the wind powers a windmill. The revolving turbine, through a series of gears, drives the propeller shaft.

The propeller itself is fixed to the end of the shaft. As the shaft turns, the propeller drives the ship through the water.

Besides the deck and engineering officers and their crewmen, there are other individuals important to the vessel's operation. These include a radio operator and a chief steward. The last named is in charge of purchasing the ship's food, and preparing and serving it. He has one or two cooks to assist him. The cooks are assisted by messmen who serve the meals and perform the clean-up chores.

Engine-room control console of the 215,000-ton *British Explorer*.

At the navigator's table

Supertankers have a "bridge aft" design, which means that the ship's control center is located toward the stern of the vessel. Tankers of this type date to the early 1960s. Before that, the tanker bridge was usually located amidships.

Locating the bridge in the afterpart of the ship is said to make for greater safety and efficiency. Since the crew is working closer to the source of shipboard power, they're better able to handle any emergency.

And deck officers have found, with the full length of the vessel in front of them as they navigate, that they have a better "feel" of the vessel. This is especially true when docking; it's easier to judge the ship's speed and angle of approach and detect any swing toward or away from dock side.

The ship's after island, where the bridge is located, usually consists of as many as seven different decks. The topmost deck, which crewmen sometimes called the "monkey island," carries signal lights and flags, radio aerials, radar scanners, and a magnetic compass. Just below is the bridge deck, where the wheelhouse is located. It's from the wheelhouse that the ship is steered and navigated. Here one finds the steering

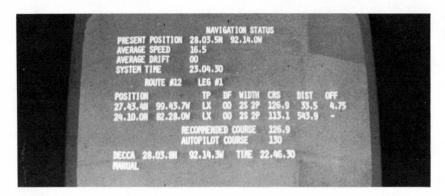

control system, the engine control and engine signal system, and a communications system that links the bridge to all parts of the ship.

The bridge also contains a chart table and navigational instruments, although sometimes these are to be found in a special compartment adjoining the wheelhouse called the chartroom.

In most supertankers, the accommodations for the ship's master, the officers, and the crew are located beneath the bridge deck. There, too, are to be found the galley, messrooms, recreation room, hobby rooms, and perhaps a darkroom for camera enthusiasts, a projection room for movies, and a library.

Below the living spaces are the ship's engine room, the boiler space, and the bunker tanks for storage of fuel. The engine room is of enormous size, perhaps as tall as a six- or seven-story building.

The various engine room units are operated from a central control room. Automatic electronic sensors and other safety devices monitor such things as boiler pressure and the temperature of propeller-shaft bearings, and the readings are reported on control-room dials and meters. The engineer on duty can tell at a glance how every piece of equipment is operating. On some of the newer vessels, engine room equipment can also be monitored on the navigating bridge.

There are two main routes that supertankers take. One follows the sea lanes between Europe and the Persian Gulf, around the Cape of Good Hope at Africa's southern tip. The other stretches between the

Persian Gulf and Japan, taking departing vessels in an easterly direction across the Indian Ocean, through the Strait of Malacca, then north northeast to Japan.

The distance from Ras Tanura, Saudi Arabia's chief port on the Gulf, to Milford Haven in Wales, is 11,300 miles. Not only is it a very long trip, it can also be—as far as most of the crew members are concerned—a painfully boring one.

When fully loaded, the average supertanker travels at a speed of 14 or 15 knots (meaning a vessel will cover 14 or 15 nautical miles in an hour; a nautical mile equals 1.15 statute miles). At this rate of speed, the voyage from Milford Haven to the Persian Gulf takes one month. It's another month going back.

"You read a lot," says one crewman. "You drink a lot of coffee. You write letters, very long letters. I carry on correspondence with people all over the world."

There's a recreation room for card playing, for checkers or chess. Ping-Pong is popular. There's a library and frequently a small swimming pool. There's television, of course, although there are only a few days of each voyage when the vessel is close enough to a transmitter to enable the set to pick up a picture. But there

Crewmen's game room aboard the *Esso Nederland*.

is also a supply of video-tape cassettes aboard, which can be played any time. They feature leading international sports events and American television programs.

Meals are hearty. Dinner includes a soup course, a choice of two entrees, mixed vegetables, fruit, cheese and crackers, and dessert. Wine is served with meals.

The food often has ethnic appeal. Italian crewmen want lasagne and other pasta dishes. With a Japanese crew, rice is a staple.

As the ship steams toward its destination, the navigator plots the vessel's course. While he has a multitude of electronic systems to assist him, he also makes use of a sextant, a navigational aid with a long tradition.

Twice every 24 hours, just before sunrise and just after sunset, the navigator uses the sextant to measure the angle of familiar stars above the horizon. This, the exact time, and other information enable him to locate the spot on the earth's surface directly below the star, known as the star's earthly position.

Using the *Nautical Almanac,* the navigator can figure out how far the ship is from the star's earthly position. He records this distance on a nautical chart. It is known as a line of position.

The navigator draws a line of position for each one of several stars. Where the lines cross is called a fix. This is the ship's position.

The navigator uses his findings to check the information being derived from the various pieces of electronic equipment. Chief among these is a long-range navigational system that is based on pulsed radio signals from shore stations. A line of position is figured from each station.

Conventional marine radio signals can be disrupted by disturbances in the ionosphere or severe weather. Crowded radio frequencies can also cause delays in getting messages transmitted. But satellite communications, which some vessels use, are not subject to such annoyances. They make for a faster, more dependable system.

Many supertankers are also equipped with collision avoidance radar. The viewing screen of an ordinary radar system displays a "blip"—a small spot of light—for each nearby ship. Collision avoidance radar does much more. The computer to which it is connected estimates the course of each nearby ship, and then projects these courses on the radar screen.

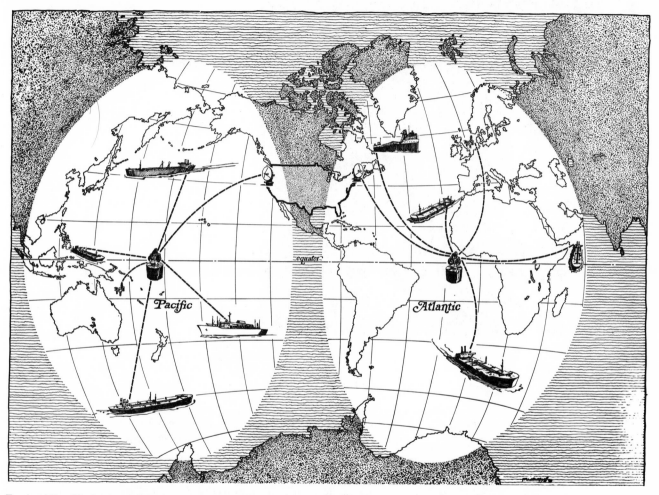

Each of the Marisat satellites—one for the Atlantic, one for the Pacific—covers an area of 60 million square miles.

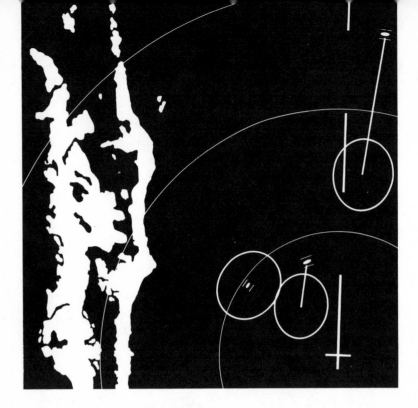

In collision avoidance radar, oval-shaped symbols represent areas of predicted danger for ship, which is indicated by cross. Land mass is at left.

If on a collision course with a particular vessel, an oval-shaped "predicted area of danger" is projected on the screen. The ship must avoid any heading that would bring it within that area.

At the end of its long and often wearying voyage, when the supertanker arrives at its destination, the vessel is likely to moor at a buoy or a man-made island some ten or twenty miles from shore. The crewmen never leave the ship. If the ship happens to be berthed in the Persian Gulf, it's likely to be so hot that they don't even go out onto the deck.

The crude is loaded through heavy, rigid hoses that connect the terminal pipelines or storage tanks with the ship's cargo spaces. Terminal pumps move the crude into the ship, or it may be loaded by means of

Ships load crude at Khar al Amaya sea island in the Persian Gulf.

Plimsoll mark indicates level to which ship can be loaded.

gravity. In such cases, the storage tanks are located at a point considerably higher than sea level, perhaps at the summit of a nearby hill. When the pipe valve is opened, the crude, responding to gravity's force, rushes into the ship.

Generally, a tanker can load an amount of crude equal to about 10 percent of its tonnage in an hour. A 200,000-ton vessel can, for example, take on approximately 20,000 tons of crude oil in an hour. The exact figure depends on the grade of crude being loaded and the efficiency of the loading facilities to which the ship is connected.

A ship taking on a load of crude oil can be put under tremendous strain unless the loading is done properly. As the oil pours in, the ship's hull is subjected to two opposing forces. One is the gravitational pull of the earth, which increases as the amount of crude oil in the tanks increases. This is opposed by the ship's buoyancy, it's tendency to remain afloat.

One force is pushing down; the other is thrusting upward. The vessel can bend, buckle, or even crack as a result.

To avoid this, the oil has to be distributed evenly throughout the tanks as it is pumped aboard. A special computer aboard the ship determines the plan of loading, establishing the order in which the tanks are to be filled.

A supertanker must be kept moving.

Tankers, like other vessels, can be loaded only to within legal limits. When the ship is taking on oil, it sinks in the water to certain lines that are marked on the hull. These are known as load lines or Plimsoll lines. The ship cannot be loaded beyond these lines.

The loading lines are named after Samuel Plimsoll, a member of the British Parliament, whose efforts to improve conditions at sea caused him to be known as "the Sailors' Friend." During the nineteenth century, it was not uncommon for shipowners to overload their vessels, hoping they would sink. Their goal was to collect the heavy insurance they had taken out on the vessel and its cargo.

After being elected to Parliament in 1868, Plimsoll campaigned for legislation that established load standards for merchant ships. When Plimsoll's bill became law, it required that every British vessel have a line painted on its hull to indicate the maximum depth to which it could be loaded. By the time Plimsoll died in 1898, every merchant marine in the world was using load lines.

As soon as the ship is loaded, it departs. Not a minute is wasted. Some sources say that it costs $30,000 a day to operate a supertanker. Other sources say that it's closer to $50,000. Whatever the amount, no owner wants his ship sitting around a port. It must be kept moving.

5/Superports

It used to be that ships were designed to be navigated within the limits of the ports they were to serve. The *Queen Elizabeth* and the *Queen Mary,* two of the most noted passenger liners in the world during the 1940s and 1950s, each had a draft of 39 1/2 feet. The depth of New York harbor, a principal port of call for these vessels, is 42 feet.

Modern supertankers changed that kind of thinking. Today the port must often be designed—or redesigned—to accommodate the ship.

A loaded 200,000-ton tanker sits 60 feet deep in the water. At the time the first supertankers went into service in the late 1960s, few ports of the world could accommodate them. They simply were not deep enough. For example, the entrance to Delaware Bay, which leads to Philadelphia and Wilmington, is no deeper than 50 feet. Freeport, Texas, one of the principal tanker ports on the Gulf of Mexico, has a channel that is a mere 35 feet in depth.

But in the past decade or so, hundreds of millions of dollars have been spent deepening ports and constructing terminal facilities around the world. Today there are more than 100 ports able to receive supertankers and handle their cargoes.

The United States—as of 1978—still had no supertanker terminal. Sites for terminals have been agreed

Worldwide deepwater terminal locations

upon, however. But supertankers won't begin calling on the United States until construction is completed, sometime during the 1980s.

Bringing a fully laden supertanker into a port and putting the vessel next to a dock is no easy matter. A big ship, even when it is moving at the rate of only a few feet per minute, wants to keep moving. A slight miscalculation and the vessel can smash the dock to pieces, crumpling its own hull plates in the process.

These problems plagued supertankers at first. They're much less severe today, thanks to docking sonar.

Tugs assist in the berthing of the *Esso Mercia* at Milford Haven, one of the world's busiest deepwater ports.

To calculate ship's movement in docking, sonar signals are sent to sea bottom.

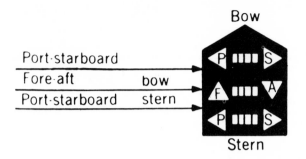

Bow

Port·starboard

Fore·aft   bow

Port·starboard   stern

Stern

The signals return to be translated by computer into a display that looks like this.

Sonar refers to an electronic system that transmits sound waves through water, then interprets the acoustic waves that bounce back. It's an acronym derived from the words SOund NAvigation Ranging. When applied to a docking operation, sonar enables the man at the controls to know exactly how fast the ship is moving in relation to the dock.

The ship sends out sonar signals to the ocean bottom. They reflect off the bottom and return to the vessel. If the ship is moving, there is a difference in the frequency between the wave sent out and the wave that comes rebounding back. This difference is interpreted by the system's electronic controls and expressed in terms of the ship's movement.

Not only does the ship's master get a report on the forward movement of the vessel, but the sonar system also tells him in what direction the ship's bow and stern are moving, and at what speeds. All speeds are expressed in terms of feet per minute.

Weather and current have no effect upon docking sonar. The waves can be distorted, however, by the temperature of the water and the amount of salt it contains (some oceans are saltier than others). But the system is able to adjust automatically for such variations, giving accurate readings in waters up to 500 to 600 feet in depth.

A supertanker doesn't necessarily have to tie up to a dock. In fact, an increasing number of tankers are loading and unloading at offshore mooring buoys. The typical buoy is circular in design, ranging from 30 to 45 feet in diameter. It resembles a giant aspirin tablet.

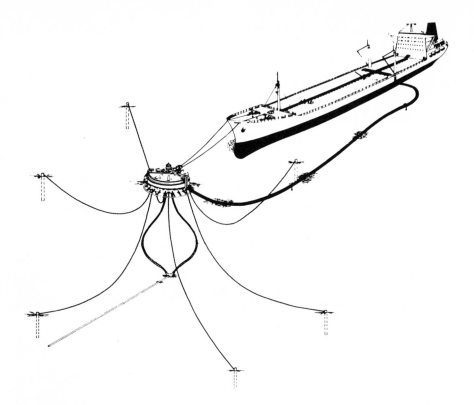

Mooring buoys for super-tankers are in widespread use today. Ship discharges cargo into floating hoses. Underwater pipeline then carries oil to storage facilities on shore.

Mooring buoys, which are connected by underwater pipelines to storage tanks on shore, can be anchored almost anywhere along a coastline, not merely where a deepwater harbor happens to be available. Several are 20 or 30 miles out at sea. The terminal facilities planned for the United States are to include such buoys.

These buoys offer a number of advantages. They save time, an important factor in the case of big tankers. Entering a harbor and maneuvering through it to ultimately tie up at a pier can take anywhere from a few hours to the better part of a day, depending on the size of the harbor and the navigational problems it presents.

Before a supertanker (or any vessel) can enter a port, it must take aboard a harbor pilot, an expert in the harbor and its characteristics, that is, its currents, turns, shoals, and shallow-water areas. A helicopter brings out the pilot to the ship. When he reaches the bridge, he takes over the navigation of the ship. The harbor pilot goes aboard again when the vessel is departing, and directs the ship until it reaches the open sea.

It's simpler when mooring to a buoy. A launch takes the ship's mooring lines to the buoy and secures them. Then the vessel hooks up to the buoy's floating hoses and pumps off its oil.

The buoy is equipped with a swivel which permits the ship to turn freely with the wind and current,

Future captain practices mooring ship model at Grenoble training center.

Anchored near Lyme Bay, England, the *Batillus* off-loads cargo to a smaller tanker.

swinging in much the same way a weather vane pivots in the wind. When the tanker leaves the buoy, the lines are let loose and the ship floats free.

In cases where there is no mooring buoy or port facilities to accommodate a supertanker, the vessel may be unloaded by a procedure known as lightering. Its crude oil is simply transferred to another, smaller, tanker at some offshore rendezvous point.

In the traditional lightering operation, the bigger ship anchors, and the lightering vessel comes alongside and ties up. Then the transfer of cargo begins. But in recent years underway lightering has been successfully carried out; that is, the cargo is transferred while both ships are in motion, steaming along at speeds of from five to seven knots. Underway lightering makes for increased speed and efficiency in the transfer of the cargo.

The most advanced superports in the world are to be found, as might be expected, in the Persian Gulf. Iran, Saudi Arabia, and Kuwait, the three major oil-exporting countries of the world, all offer supertanker

Tokyo Maru takes on a cargo of crude oil at Ras Tanura, Saudi Arabia.

terminals capable of handling the biggest vessels. Iran's chief port is Kharg Island, located deep within the Gulf, almost at the extreme northern end. Saudi Arabia offers Ras Tanura, and Kuwait loads tankers at Mina-al-Ahmadi.

Even the smaller producing nations—Abu Dhabi, Qatar, Oman, and Dubai—have modern terminal facilities for supertankers.

Continental Europe gets its supply of Middle Eastern crude oil through an abundance of superports, almost 30 of them. Many of Europe's oil refineries are located in or near the major port cities.

The Dutch city of Rotterdam is the biggest oil port in the world, receiving more crude than any other. Located within the deltas of the Rhine and Maas rivers, Rotterdam has been important as a port for well over a hundred years. What is called the "New Waterway" was constructed at the beginning of the nineteenth century, providing Rotterdam with a direct, open link to the sea.

The channel has been widened and deepened through the years. Today, Rotterdam can handle 400,000-ton tankers with ease.

Rotterdam has also become notable as an industrial center. Big shipyards are located there. After World War II, oil refineries were built within the city, and today Rotterdam ranks as Europe's leading petrochemical center.

Oil unloaded at Rotterdam goes to supply the refineries within the harbor area, or it may be piped to refineries in Amsterdam or the Belgian city of Antwerp. Some supertankers arriving in Rotterdam discharge their crude into smaller tankers which supply other refineries in northwestern Europe.

North and east of Rotterdam, Germany offers a supertanker port at Wilhelmshaven, also on the North Sea. Pipelines from Wilhelmshaven carry the crude to German refineries in the Ruhr Valley. Northwestern Europe also receives Middle Eastern crude at the French port of Antifer near Le Havre on the English Channel. Pipelines from Le Havre follow the course of the Seine Valley—Le Havre is at the mouth of the Seine—to supply French refineries. Antifer is capable of handling the biggest supertankers, fully laden 500,000-tonners.

Besides its tremendous port facilities, Rotterdam is a major shipbuilding center. Here 225,000-ton *Esso Cambria* is launched.

Fos-sur-Mer in France is another major European terminal for supertankers.

Many other European superports are on the Mediterranean Sea. Among the biggest of these is Fos-sur-Mer in France at the mouth of the Rhone River near Marseille. One of the first European ports to handle 300,000-ton vessels, Fos-sur-Mer feeds refineries, not only in France, but in Switzerland and West Germany as well.

For several years, Great Britain's chief superport has been Milford Haven in Wales. The water at Milford, one of the world's finest natural harbors, is very deep, and 300,000-ton vessels can put in there. In southwest Ireland, there's Bantry Bay, where 330,000-ton tankers discharge their crude. It is then transshipped in smaller tankers to refineries in western Europe.

Italy boasts no fewer than nine superports. An offshore island at Genoa can handle 500,000-ton vessels. Genoa supplies Italy, West Germany, and Switzerland with crude.

The deepwater fjords of Norway have been adapted to provide berths for supertankers. Norway has three superports; Sweden, two of them.

Japan, with no oil of its own, is totally dependent on foreign imports. Thus, superports are common in Japan.

Tokyo Bay is to Japan what Rotterdam is to western Europe. There are three superports within Tokyo Bay—at Chiba, Yokohama, and Kawasaki—and each can handle 250,000-ton vessels. There are four other major ports in Japan along the south coast of the island of Honshu. And at Okinawa in the southern Ryukyu Islands, 300,000-ton supertankers can be accommodated.

International oil, banking, and industrial interests are eyeing a number of the islands of Micronesia and Southeast Asia with the idea of establishing a network of oil storage and transshipment stations for supertankers. Oil on its way from the Middle East to Japan would be moved to one of these Pacific ports in 500,000-ton tankers, then ferried to Japan in smaller ships.

The first of these terminals was proposed in 1977 for the Palau Islands. The Palau Islands are a group of about 200 islands within the Caroline Islands, located due east of the Philippines. Included in the United States Trust Territory of the Pacific, the Carolines are administered by the Department of the Interior under a mandate from the United Nations.

The terminal would be located within Kossol Harbor at the island of Badeldaob in northern Palau. It would be called Port Pacific. Protected by reefs and with water deep enough to accommodate one-million-ton vessels, Kossol Harbor is bigger than the harbors of New York or Rotterdam.

Other sites that have been proposed for Pacific superports include Lombok Island in Indonesia, and southern Thailand. By using these sites, tankers would be able to avoid the Malacca Strait between Sumatra and Malaysia. These countries, fearful of oil spills, have sought to limit tanker traffic in the Strait.

A supertanker terminal such as Port Pacific, with its huge tank farm, would allow oil to be stockpiled. When the oil-producing nations put an embargo on oil in 1973, Japan was sent reeling. Stockpiling would help the country ride out a temporary interruption of imports.

When plans to build superports on remote Pacific Islands were announced, it triggered another confrontation between oil interests and environmentalists. The waters surrounding the Palau Islands teem

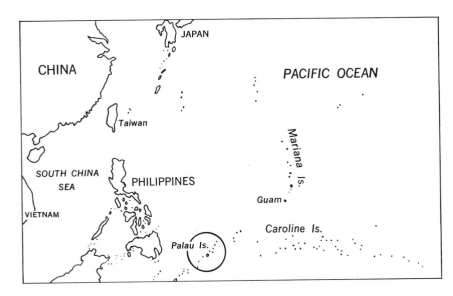

with coral and marine life, including 20-foot crocodiles and a poisonous sea snake that is worshiped as a local god. Dredging and blasting in connection with the construction of port facilities would be certain to destroy vast areas of coral, the breeding ground for marine life. Opposition is also based on the fear of a drastic change in the traditional ways of life. "The superport would be an environmental disaster of the worst order," Robert Owen, chief conservation officer of the U.S. Trust Territory and a resident of Palau for twenty-seven years, told *The New York Times*. "The people would trade a few years of money for their whole fragile environment and culture."

Roman Tmetuchl, a local businessman, expressed an opposition viewpoint, saying, "The world has always had pollution and been able to overcome it. These people [the environmentalists] want to keep Palau a human zoo so they can come and swim and take pretty pictures and then go home to their own lives, while the people here without work starve."

Should the Kossol Harbor terminal become a reality, it could render Palau the energy hub of the Pacific.

Worldwide Superports

PORT	Estimated maximum vessel size in DWT
AFRICA	
CANARY ISLANDS	
Tenerife	200,000
CONGO	
Djeno	250,000
LIBYA	
Es Sider	210,000
Marsa el Brega	300,000
Ras Lanuf	355,000
Zuetina	250,000
MOROCCO	
Mohammedia	100,000
NIGERIA	
Bonny	375,000
Brass River	250,000
Escravos	350,000
Forcados	250,000
SOUTH AFRICA	
Durban	210,000
ASIA-PACIFIC	
BRUNEI	
Seria	250,000
INDONESIA	
Ardjuna	200,000
Jatibarang	200,000
JAPAN	
Atsumi	200,000
Chiba	250,000
Kawasaki	250,000
Kiire	500,000
Niigata	280,000
Olta	250,000
Okinawa	500,000
Shimotsu	250,000
Tokuyama	250,000
Ube	200,000
Yokkaichi	300,000
Yokohama	300,000
SINGAPORE	
Pulum Bukom	200,000
SOUTH KOREA	
Ulsan	200,000
EUROPE	
FRANCE	
Antifer	250,000
Fos-sur-Mer	280,000
Sète	275,000
GREECE	
Aghil Theodori	250,000
IRELAND	
Bantry Bay	330,000
ITALY	
Ancona	300,000
Augusta	280,000
Gaeta	250,000
Gela	500,000
Genoa	500,000
Milazzo	330,000
Porto Torres	300,000
Savona	250,000
Taranto	210,000
NETHERLANDS	
Rotterdam	400,000
NORWAY	
Mongstad	300,000
Slagenragen	250,000
SPAIN	
Algeciras	250,000
Bilbao	500,000
Cartagena	260,000
Málaga	300,000
SWEDEN	
Brofjorden	500,000
Göteborg	225,000
Lysekil	350,000
UNITED KINGDOM	
Finnart	330,000
Milford Haven	250,000
WEST GERMANY	
Wilhelmshaven	250,000

MIDDLE EAST

ABU DHABI
Das Island 250,000

DUBAI
Fateh 300,000

IRAN
Kharg Island 500,000
Lavan Island 220,000

IRAQ
Mina-al-Bakir 350,000
Ras Bahregan 250,000

ISRAEL
Eilat 350,000

KUWAIT
Mena-el-Ahmadi 400,000

OMAN
Mena al Fahal 320,000

QATAR
Halul Island 500,000
Umm Said 300,000

SAUDI ARABIA
Ju Aymah 500,000
Ras Tanura 500,000

TURKEY
Izmit 250,000

NORTH AMERICA

CANADA
Come-by-Chance 320,000
Point Tupper 350,000
Port Hawkesbury 350,000
Saint John 350,000

SOUTH AMERICA

BAHAMAS
Freeport 380,000

BRAZIL
São Franciscodusul 200,000
São Sebastio 300,000

CHILE
Quintero Bay 210,000

NETHERLANDS ANTILLES
Aruba 285,000
Bonaire 500,000
Bullen Bay 500,000
Curaço 500,000

TRINIDAD
Galeota Point 250,000
Pointe-a-Pierre 260,000

This is Canso Strait, leading to Port Hawkesbury in Nova Scotia, one of Canada's principal superports.

Palau lies only 500 miles east of Manila, 1,000 miles north of Sydney, Australia, and 2,000 miles south of Tokyo Bay. Some sources say oil might even be transshipped from Palau to the United States.

As of 1978, the only supertanker terminals in North America were to be found in Canada—at Saint John, New Brunswick; Point Tupper and Come-by-Chance, Newfoundland; and Port Hawkesbury, Nova Scotia. With harbor depths of up to 100 feet, Port Hawkesbury holds the distinction of having served as port for the largest ship ever to dock in North America, the 326,000-ton *Universe Japan*.

Some crude oil bound for the United States is first shipped to Port Hawkesbury. But most American supplies go first to the Caribbean area. The islands of Trinidad; Grand Bahama in the Bahamas; and Aruba, Bonaire, and Curaçao in the Netherlands Antilles all offer terminals for supertankers. Smaller tankers ferry the crude to the United States.

As all of this implies, the United States has dragged its feet in constructing supertanker terminals. There are several sites on the East Coast where the water is deep enough to accommodate supertankers. These are to be found off the coast of Maine near Eastport, far to the north in the state. Portland, Maine, near the New Hampshire border, has water that is deep enough, too. Terminal facilities would have to be built in both locations.

In the case of the prospective supertanker port at Eastport, the lack of a terminal is not the only problem. Ships must pass through Canadian waters when approaching the port. An agreement with Canadian authorities would have to be hammered out before the Eastport site could be developed.

On the West Coast, Puget Sound in northwestern Washington offers water deep enough to handle supertankers. But don't look for supertankers in Puget Sound within the near future. The state of Washington passed a law in 1975 that bans tankers of more than 125,000 tons from entering the Sound. (The subject of whether a state has the legal right to pass legislation regulating oil tankers on the waterways is before the Supreme Court.)

The Port of Valdez in Alaska, a protected fjord about 12 miles long and 2 1/2 miles wide, is the terminal to which crude oil from the North Slope flows. The berths at Valdez can handle 165,000-ton ships. With the addition of mooring points, however, 250,000-ton vessels could be accommodated.

A recent proposal concerns a pair of offshore terminals in the Gulf of Mexico. These sites won the approval of the Department of Transportation in 1976. One of the approved sites is located 18 miles offshore, south of Grand Island, Louisiana, and would pump crude to refineries in Louisiana, Mississippi, and the Midwest. It is known as LOOP (for Louisiana offshore oil port).

The *Universe Japan*, 326,000 tons, in Canso Strait. Ship is largest ever to dock in North American port.

The other site, called Seadock, is located 26 miles south and east of Freeport, Texas. It would supply crude to refineries along the Gulf Coast and in the Midwest.

The Seadock complex, to be constructed in water 100 feet deep, is to consist of several mooring buoys, all of which would be connected to an offshore pumping platform. The platform would be linked by an underwater pipeline to oil storage facilities on shore, near Freeport.

After mooring at a buoy, a tanker would hook up to floating hoses and pump off its oil to the offshore platform. The oil would then be moved from the platform to the storage tanks on shore.

Seadock would be capable of handling 2 1/2 million barrels of oil a day, almost 15 percent of the country's daily petroleum requirements. The facility could be expanded to handle 4 million barrels a day.

The Loop project would be similar, that is, it would consist of several mooring buoys and an offshore pumping platform. Loop would be able to handle about 3 1/2 million barrels of oil a day.

Loop and Seadock are enormous undertakings. Each would cost several hundred million dollars. Several years of construction are involved. Until one of these projects is completed, the supertanker, as far as the United States is concerned, is a ship without a port.

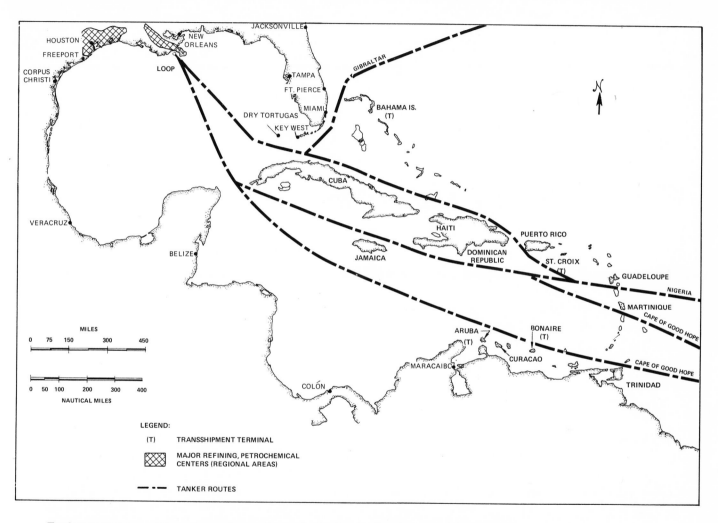

Tanker routes to and from Loop deepwater port. Routes for Seadock would be similar.

6/Oil and Water

Bantry Bay in Ireland's southwestern corner is one of the most beautiful, most admired stretches of seacoast in all of Europe. It also provides one of the finest natural harbors in the world, with the water running to depths of over 100 feet.

In 1968, Bantry Bay became the site of a huge Gulf Oil depot and transshipment terminal, with a half-mile long jetty providing docking facilities for a fleet of 330,000-ton supertankers. A million-ton capacity tank farm was built on Whiddy Island at the bay's end. Supertankers entering the bay have their cargo moved to the storage tanks on Whiddy Island or pumped into smaller "shuttle" tankers that carry the crude to other European ports.

The tanker traffic at Bantry Bay never stops. Some ships are always unloading, while others are loading, and still others wait at anchor.

Late one October afternoon in 1974, the 93,000-ton tanker *Universe Leader* began taking on a load of crude oil destined for Spain. At some unknown time and for some unknown interval, a 16-inch sea valve 30 feet below the waterline was left open, and oil under tremendous pressure began spewing into the Bay.

Estimates vary as to how much oil was spilled. Pollution officials in Ireland put the amount at 25,000 barrels. British newspapers said 30,000 barrels. An American magazine said the amount was twice that.

Whatever the figure, the results were horrendous. Oil covered 22 miles of shoreline and forced three fishing villages to close down. Some 35,000 gallons of oil were removed from the water's surface at the tiny village of Gerahies, about four miles from the Whiddy Island terminal. And at the village of Gornakilty, several miles farther on, conditions were even worse.

The size of the spill was all that was exceptional about it. The fact that a spill had occurred wasn't. Gulf once acknowledged that 23 oil spills had taken place in its first seven years of operation at Bantry Bay.

"Environmental dangers inevitably trail after oil, wherever and however it is transported," a recent joint report by three committees of the United States declared. Operations at tanker terminals during loading and unloading are only one of the causes of spills and the environmental dangers that can result. Spills also stem from normal tanker operations, that is, tank washing and deballasting (explained later in this chapter). There are also the spills that result from tanker accidents.

In any spill, the amount of oil involved is of overriding importance in attempting to estimate the amount

Oil spill menaces a strip of Florida coastline.

During tanker unloading operations, floating barrier like this one can serve as "first line of defense," holding spilled oil in check.

of damage. But there are other factors to be considered. Where the spill occurred is important, too. A great deal of spilled oil in a small and enclosed area is going to be much more damaging than the same amount of oil spread over a larger area.

The prevailing weather conditions at the time of the spill and the state of the tides and currents also have to be considered. The type of oil spilled has an effect, too. Generally speaking, crude oil is less hazardous to the environment than most types of fuel oil.

Finally, the efficiency of the clean-up operations have to be weighed. The work of cleaning up a spill usually begins with an effort to contain it. In harbors, floating containment barriers, called booms, are used

Coast Guard crewmen rig a containment barrier to surround an oil spill.

to encircle the spill and hold it in check until it can be removed by vacuum pumps or mechanical skimmers. In the open ocean, of course, such methods usually aren't practical.

Spilled oil can wreak terrible environmental damage. Waterfowl and other birds are the immediate victims. Shellfish and fin fish can also die. Marine plant life is destroyed. Marine mammals are threatened.

But some scientists say that the environmental damage caused by oil spills is merely a temporary condition. They say that oil wastes discharged into the sea are converted to harmless elements by sea bacteria. "An environmental balance exists in the oceans," according to Carl H. Oppenheimer, a professor of Marine Sciences and Microbiology at the University of Texas, "whereby oil is continually being decomposed by microorganisms; otherwise, the earth would be knee-deep in oil from natural products."

There is evidence to support this theory. Three ocean engineers at the Massachusetts Institute of

In spills near coastal areas, waterfowl and other birds are often the first victims.

Straw "mops" are sometimes used to soak up spilled oil.

Technology spent eighteen months studying how the Atlantic Coast shorelands were affected by the sinking of oil tankers during World War II. Between January and June, 1942, German submarines torpedoed 100 merchant ships on the Atlantic Ocean, causing the spillage of 20 million barrels of oil.

The study was released in 1977. The engineers concluded that the environmental impact had been minor. "I think we proved that we needn't panic every time there's an oil spill," said one researcher.

Seawater does contain bacteria and microorganisms that work to decompose petroleum, but the process

Oil congeals in cold weather; decomposition is retarded.

is a slow one and depends on the type and amount of oil involved. It also depends on the water temperature. Decomposition occurs much faster in warm water. In the area of the world where the water is close to freezing or sheeted with ice, decomposition is a sluggish process. Oil pollution is now evident in remote regions of the Arctic and Antarctic, far from any tanker routes.

Anyone who has visited an ocean beach in recent years is likely to have encountered one of the more offensive forms of oil pollution. It's oil that washes up onto beaches in black gooey globs, each more or less the size of a tennis ball. Get some of this oil on your hand or foot and it's almost as difficult to remove as tar from a city street.

Tankers can cause this type of pollution by washing their tanks. After a tanker has discharged its cargo, the inside walls of the ship's tanks remain coated with a thick oil residue, and globs of crude lie on the tank bottoms.

Cleaning this sludge away is done automatically. The tanks are sealed and streams of water at high velocity from built-in nozzles reach into every corner and crevice of the tanks. There are as many as five to ten washers for each tank, a hundred or more for the entire ship. The job takes several hours.

Once the tanks are clean, the problem is what to do with the wash water. Standard procedure for many years has been to pump it into the ocean. Of course, all of the oily residue goes with it, and much of it eventually washes up on beaches.

The same thing happens during what are referred to as deballasting operations. During the voyage to the Persian Gulf, or any time they're empty, tankers take on seawater and store it in their cargo tanks to give the ship added stability.

Without such ballast, the ship would ride so high in the water, it would be difficult to maneuver. As the vessel nears the port where it is to take on its cargo, it discharges the seawater. Oil still remaining in the tanks goes into the sea, too.

While these operations involve only leftover oil, the amounts are sizeable. It has been estimated that the oil residue remaining in a tanker after it has pumped off its cargo can amount to 1/2 of 1 percent of the ship's capacity. With a tanker that is 250,000 tons in size, that means the leftover oil can amount to 1,250 tons.

Consider that hundreds of tankers, big and small, are in operation, and each must carry out washing and deballasting operations; obviously, millions of tons of oil are involved. Besides the pollution, there's the loss of oil, a wastage that could run to as much as $1 billion a year, according to industry estimates.

One partial solution to the problem, as it concerns tank washing, is what is called the LOT (for load on top) system of discharging the wash water and ballast water. Before the mixture of oil and water is pumped out, it is allowed to settle. The oil, being lighter, rises to lie on top of the water. Then the water is discharged from beneath the oil. The layer of oil, which eventually comes to rest on the tank bottom, is kept on board, and the new cargo is pumped in on top of it.

When empty, tankers ride high. They take on seawater—ballast—to increase stability.

Tank-washing machine

The load-on-top method of tank washing came into widespread use during the mid-1960s. It is estimated that tankers representing about 80 percent of all tanker tonnage use LOT today.

But it is not a perfect system. In order to be effective, it requires a reasonably long voyage; otherwise, there might not be sufficient time for the oil-water mixture to settle and separate. Rough seas buffeting the ship can delay the settling too. There can also be difficulty in determining precisely when the oil level has been reached. As the pumps keep pumping and pumping, some oil is discharged into the sea.

Because of these difficulties, some tankers have adopted a waterless washing method. Instead of water, a portion of the tanker's cargo of crude is used. At the time the vessel is being unloaded, the high pressure sprays send crude oil careening against the tank sides. Crude oil has actually been proven to be more efficient than seawater in dissolving the sludge.

The crude used in washing is simply pumped out along with the cargo load. One company, Exxon, is equipping all of its supertankers with crude oil washing systems.

A method has also been devised to solve the pollution problem that results from deballasting operations. It involves the installation of separate tanks to carry the ballast water. Oil never goes into them. But since such tanks can cut the amount of cargo space by as much as 10 or 15 percent, tanker owners are reluctant to install them.

Spilled oil and the resulting pollution is not the only problem associated with washing and deballasting operations. One ghastly 16-day period late in 1969 is evidence of this.

On December 15, 1969, the 206,000-ton *Marpessa,* steaming off Senegal on her maiden voyage, experienced a tank explosion and sank. Two crewmen lost their lives.

Just two weeks later, a sister ship, the *Mactra,* while in the Mozambique Channel, between the West African coast and Madagascar, also suffered a tank explosion, but managed to limp into port. Again, two men were killed.

The very next day, off Liberia, a 220,000-ton Norwegian tanker, the *Kong Haakan VII,* was ripped by a tank explosion. Like the *Mactra,* the *Kong Haakan VII* managed to reach port.

In the months that followed, investigators representing the oil companies involved and the shipowners and their insurers sought to determine what caused the explosions. The entire concept of supertankers was in jeopardy. There were at the time 63 tankers of 200,000 tons or more in service, and more than 300 others were in various stages of construction. But if supertankers were to be regarded as floating time bombs, no one would ever purchase one, insure one, or sail aboard such a vessel.

The investigations continued for more than two years. One fact was established right away. Each of the three ships had been cleaning its tanks when the explosions had occurred.

Contrary to what most people believe, a supertanker is safest when it is fully loaded. Tankers have been ravaged by fire, their superstructures destroyed, yet their cargo, sealed tightly in the ship's tanks, has remained intact.

It is not the crude oil itself that represents a hazard, but the vapor given off by it. After a tanker has discharged its cargo, the oily residue remaining in the tanks exudes hydrocarbon vapor in great volume.

But at this stage, the gas cannot explode because it is in an "overrich" state, meaning that there isn't sufficient oxygen present to enable the gas to ignite. Drop a lighted match in a smoke-filled jar, and the match will go out before it strikes the jar bottom. The same principle applies in a tanker right after the crude has been pumped out. There's not enough oxygen present to sustain combustion.

It's when fresh air enters the tanks and the overrich atmosphere begins to dissipate that the tanks can become highly explosive. The vapor can then be touched off by the tiniest spark. The faint spark that results when a wrench is dropped on a steel deck or even the static electric sparks discharged by a nylon shirt can do the job.

Something of this nature caused the explosions that ripped apart the *Marpessa, Mactra,* and *Kong Haakan VII.* The investigators found that the explosions might even have been created by the tank-washing operation itself, by the powerful jets of water slamming into the tank sides. One set of experiments showed that water jetting out of high velocity nozzles picked up static electricity in its flight, and discharged this electricity upon striking tank metal surfaces.

Meanwhile, oil companies were at work seeking methods to prevent explosions from taking place. Their efforts concentrated on the removal of oxygen from the tanks.

The method finally developed involves the use of gases from the ship's boiler. These gases, called flue gases, are high in carbon dioxide content. Carbon dioxide will not burn. It is the gas used in fire extinguishers.

The gas is drawn from the ship's funnel, cooled, and scrubbed, and then pumped into the cargo tanks as the oil is being pumped out. The hydrocarbon vapor remains at an overrich level, and thus no explosion can take place.

This gas-inerting system, as it is called, is in widespread use today, and is believed to have solved the problem of tank explosions. Virtually all supertankers are equipped with such systems, and U.S. Coast Guard regulations require gas-inerting now for tankers of 100,000 tons or larger that fly the American flag.

Tanker crewman checks gauge readings on pump delivering inert gas to cargo tanks.

Oil pollution of the seas is not a new problem. As far back as 1925, the federal government conducted a pollution prevention experiment involving a tanker named the *Charles Pratt*. The vessel was fitted with a device that skimmed oil from seawater during deballasting operations.

Attempts to control pollution through legislation go back even further. In 1922, the British passed the Oil in Navigable Waters Act, and in 1926 the Pollution of the Sea by Oil Act became the law in the United States.

The problem was attacked on an international basis in 1954. A conference in London, the recommendations of which were later ratified by the United States and many other nations, established prescribed zones of the sea within which oily discharges were prohibited.

More recently, regulations for tanker operation have been established by the Intergovernmental Maritime Consultative Organization—IMCO—with headquarters in London. A United Nations Organization, it consists of just over 100 member nations. They meet regularly to discuss such topics as oil discharges at sea, ship construction standards, traffic control in congested areas, and personnel safety.

IMCO sponsored the International Convention for the Prevention of Pollution at Sea in 1973, which sought to broaden and strengthen international regulations. The United States has not ratified the recommendations of the Convention, however.

Under the terms of the Ports and Waterways Safety Act of 1972, the Coast Guard has been given the authority to require vessels entering U.S. waters to maintain certain standards as far as design and equipment are concerned. The Coast Guard can fine vessel owners for violating these standards, or bar any vessel from entering U.S. waters.

After a rash of tanker accidents late in 1976, Congress moved to enact stricter tanker safety standards and traffic control procedures. These were aimed, not at supertankers, but at the ever-increasing number of smaller tankers entering U.S. ports, often older, poorly-manned vessels.

These tankers were described in 1977 as " . . . old crocks that have outlived their usefulness," by Howard F. Casey, deputy assistant secretary of maritime affairs for the U.S. Maritime Administration. "There's some right old rubbish afloat," an oil company executive agrees. These "rust buckets," as they have been called, are the subject of the next chapter.

7/Troubled Tankers

During the late 1970s, as United States oil imports went higher and higher, the number of tanker accidents kept increasing. The year 1976 was, up to that time, the worst ever in terms of tanker mishaps. A total of 19 tankers went aground, sank, or blew up during 1976.

The final month of the year was particularly grim. Consider:

• On December 15, the *Argo Merchant* ran aground 28 miles southeast of Nantucket Island, and within a week broke up, spilling most of its 200,000-barrel cargo of heavy heating oil into the sea.

• On December 17, the *Sansinena,* moored at an oil terminal in San Pedro, California, harbor, suffered a massive explosion that blew the ship apart. Eight were killed, nearly 50 injured. Between 250 and 500 barrels of fuel oil were spilled into the harbor.

• On December 24, the *Oswego Peace,* unloading cargo on the Thames River in New London, Connecticut, leaked more than 100 barrels of its own fuel oil into the river.

• On December 27, the fully laden *Olympic Games* went aground in the Delaware River, puncturing a cargo tank and spilling 3,500 barrels of crude oil.

• On December 28, the *Daphne,* carrying 420,000 barrels of crude oil, went aground off San Juan, Puerto Rico, but no oil was spilled.

• On December 31, the last radio dispatch was received from the *Grand Zenith,* bound for a generating station near Fall River, Massachusetts, carrying 200,000 barrels of oil. The vessel encountered heavy seas south of Nova Scotia and was presumed to have sunk.

A national magazine called it "a seaborne demolition derby." But none of the vessels cited above was a supertanker.

Because no United States ports are capable of accommodating the biggest tankers, the oil that America

Coast Guard helicopter hovers over *Argo Merchant,* aground off Nantucket Island.

Broken halves of *Argo Merchant* swirl about before sinking. About 200,000 barrels of oil were spilled.

imports has to be carried in an assortment of smaller vessels, many of which have reached old age, and are often poorly equipped and casually operated. Because they are smaller, many more of them are required.

The situation makes for crowded sea lanes and crowded ports, and crowding makes for hazards. Imagine the swarm of aircraft that would be occupying the airspace above the nation's major airports if the size of planes never advanced beyond what was available in the late 1950s.

During that period, which was before the advent of jet aircraft, the biggest planes offered by the airlines were Douglas' DC-7s and Lockheed's Constellations, both of which were four-engined piston craft. Each of these planes carried from one-fourth to one-third the number of passengers that can be carried by a modern jet.

If jet aircraft were not permitted to land at airfields in the United States today, it would mean that three

Tanker *Spartan Lady* lists heavily to port before breaking apart and sinking 150 miles outside New York harbor. Incident occurred in 1975.

Only the bow and stern of the *Sansinena* are visible after explosion tore vessel apart. Note oil containment barriers in background.

Tanker *Esso Brussels* was at anchor in New York harbor in 1973 when rammed by another ship. This enormous hole was ripped in tanker's hull.

or four times more planes would be necessary. The sky would be dark with passenger aircraft. That is somewhat the situation that exists in the United States as far as tankers are concerned.

Not only are there many more tankers than necessary entering United States waters, but they are often aging vessels, lacking in seaworthiness. "We are the garbage dump of tankers of the world," says Jess Calhoun, president of the National Marine Engineer Beneficial Association.

A tanker can become dilapidated in a relatively short span of time. Tankers are subject to deterioration because of the corrosive action of some types of oil. Oil contains sulphur. When the oil is pumped out of the ship's tanks, it leaves behind sulfur dioxide in gaseous form. The gas can condense on the interior walls of the tanks to form sulfuric acid, which is so corrosive that it eats away at the hull's steel plates. Noel Mostert, in his book *Supership,* said that a tanker can lose as much as 2 percent of its steel every year because of corrosion.

The corrosion does not occur evenly over the ship's interior. Instead, small indentations are eaten in the steel. A heavily corroded steel plate can resemble a plaster wall that's been sprayed with a blast of buckshot. When serious corrosion takes place, the affected plates must be removed and replaced, an expensive task. Not every shipowner is willing to do this.

Not only may a tanker be in a decrepit state because of poor maintenance and lack of repairs, it may also lack certain types of navigational equipment. Or its crew may be poorly trained and lacking in experience. One or all of these factors usually plays a part in any tanker mishap.

Beginning in June, 1977, the Coast Guard sought to reduce tanker accidents by requiring that vessels entering U.S. waters be equipped with certain basic navigational aids—a gyrocompass, a magnetic compass, a depth finder, a radio direction finder, and radar. Supertankers, with their modern, electronic navigation systems, far surpass Coast Guard requirements.

Another solution would be to make available official records of tanker performance, a sort of "report card" on each vessel permitted to use American ports. These records would contain information on ship maintenance and repair and report on the vessel's success—or lack of it—in meeting operational schedules.

It would list any groundings, collisions, or other mishaps in which the vessel might have been involved. As it is now, such data is not released unless the vessel's owner gives permission.

If information like this were made available, those firms chartering tankers could avoid accident-prone vessels. They could seek out the ships with the best performance records.

This information could also be made available to port authorities. A tanker with a poor record would be required to take additional precautions as it entered a port, restricting its movement to the most favorable periods, that is, when conditions of wind, tide, and current were advantageous. And when the ship did move, it would be required to use more than the usual number of tugs.

Arthur McKenzie, Director of the Tanker Advisory Service, points out that the *Argo Merchant,* mentioned above, which ran aground off Nantucket Island in December, 1976, had, in the previous 36-month period, been out of operation almost 40 percent of the time because of accidents involving the ship and repair work that had to be performed as a result. *The New York Times* called the *Argo Merchant* a "dangerous and defective ship." "Would anyone," asks McKenzie, "have used that vessel to carry our cargoes if we had known the record?"

Air traffic centers at airports throughout the United States control aircraft landings and departures. A similar system has been suggested for crowded ship passages—the Cape of Good Hope, the English Channel, the Strait of Malacca, and the Strait of Gibraltar. "What is visualized for this situation," said Noel Mostert in *Supership,* "is that all shipping will be monitored by shore stations as it steams up to certain offshore limits . . . and that, as a vessel comes within certain range, it will be given a number and a course which, fed into its own computerized system, will put the navigation under shore control."

The U.S. Coast Guard already operates such a system—but, unfortunately, only on a very limited basis. Known as VTS—for Vessel Traffic Service—the system requires that before entering certain harbors, each vessel must report to a control center its name, cargo, destination, estimated time of arrival, and other information. Once within the harbor, the vessel then reports to the control center from each one of several checkpoints. At the same time, the center keeps the vessel notified of the location and movement of other vessels and any potential hazards.

As of 1978, only San Francisco, Puget Sound, and the Houston ship channel were equipped with VTS. Installations were planned for New York, New Orleans, and Prince William Sound, which leads to the

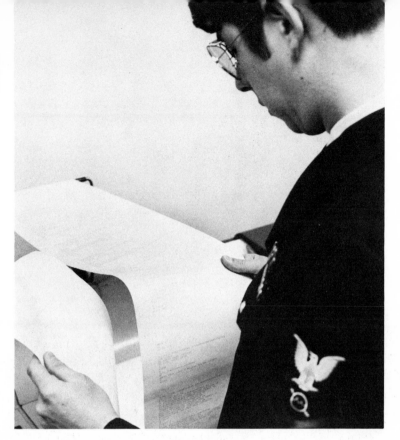

Alaskan port of Valdez. By contrast, many foreign ports, Rotterdam, Hamburg, and Liverpool, to name only three, have had some form of VTS since the mid-1960s.

There is widespread agreement that VTS should be improved and extended. "The federal government spends billions on controlling passenger aircraft," one oil company executive points out. "We should be just as willing to regulate the flow of tankers and other merchant ships in and out of our port cities."

127

Monrovia, Liberia's capital city, is the name blazoned on a thousand tankers the world over.

Much of the criticism surrounding oil and its transport has to be with the fact that a great number of tankers entering U.S. ports are registered under the Liberian flag. It is a fact that Liberia, a West African nation about the size of the state of Ohio, and without a natural harbor of its own, operates the world's largest tanker fleet.

If the next ship you chance to see in a U.S. port happens to be flying the red, white, and blue Liberian flag, it is no accident. Of the oil imported by the United States, approximately 94 percent is brought in aboard foreign-flag vessels, and about one-third of these vessels are of Liberian registry.

Money is the chief reason. A tanker (or any other vessel) registered in the United States must carry an American crew, and American labor is high-priced. A 32-man crew of Americans costs a shipowner about $1.7 million a year.

But when a tanker carries the Liberian flag, a shipowner can hire a crew of any nationality. And foreign crews do not demand as much money as American crews. For example, an all-Italian crew of 32 men costs a shipowner much less than half of what Americans must be paid—about $600,000 a year. An all-British crew receives $500,000 a year; an all-Greek crew, $325,000 a year.

An American-registered ship is also required to use American shipyards for maintenance and repair work, and it costs much more to use an American yard than a foreign one. Insurance costs for an American-registered ship are about twice as much as those for a foreign-flag vessel.

Registering the ships of foreign shipowners is profitable for Liberia. The fees that the country receives make up about 8 percent of the total goods and services produced by the nation.

Liberia is not the only nation to offer shipowners a "flag of convenience," as it is called. Panama, Cyprus, and Malaysia are some others.

Those who criticize the flag-of-convenience system say that it permits the operation of dangerously maintained ships that are manned by poorly trained crews. Of the six ships mentioned in the opening paragraphs of this chapter, five, including the *Argo Merchant,* were registered under the Liberian flag. The sixth was of Panamanian registry.

Robert J. Blackwell, an official of the U.S. Maritime Administration, testifying before a Senate

Committee, described operators of flag-of-convenience ships in these terms: "Many are out to make the cheapest buck, to put on the cheapest crews. They avoid maintaining these vessels."

But such criticism isn't quite fair.

Early in 1977, the Tanker Advisory Center published statistics showing the number of tanker losses suffered by leading maritime nations of the world for a 13-year period beginning in 1964. Loss ratios, in which the number of losses was compared to the total amount of tonnage registered by the nation, were also given. Here are the statistics:

RANKING	FLAG	NO. OF LOSSES	RATIO TO TOTAL TONNAGE (%)
1	Russian	0	.00
2	West German	1	.05
3	French	3	.06
4	Japanese	3	.06
5	British	11	.12
6	American	9	.15
7	Swedish	1	.17
8	Danish	1	.26
9	Norwegian	18	.27
10	Liberian	68	.50
11	Panamanian	17	.51
12	Spanish	3	.58
13	Italian	9	.64
14	Netherlands	2	.70
15	Greek	26	.76

As the chart indicates, Liberia's record is not the worst. While that nation had more tanker losses than any other during the period analyzed, its rate of loss was less than that of five other nations, four of them traditional maritime nations.

There is no disputing the fact that a number of vessels that fly the Liberian flag are "rust buckets" and have woeful operating records. But Liberian-registered ships also include many that are equipped with sophisticated navigational systems and that are manned by well-trained and experienced crews. When it comes to tanker groundings and collisions, the flag-of-convenience nations should not be made to shoulder all the blame.

Supertankers have had their share of accidents. Take the case of the *Metula*, a 206,000-ton vessel operated by Royal Dutch Shell. Early in August, 1974, the *Metula* went aground in the Strait of Magellan

Oil from the grounded *Metula* is off-loaded to the smaller tanker, *Harvella*.

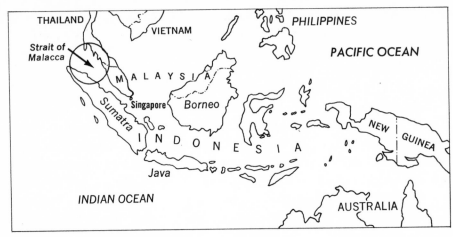

at the southern tip of South America, said to be one of the world's richest marine life areas. Oil poured out of the ship's ruptured tanks, creating an oil slick that was 65 miles long. Many Chilean beaches were fouled with oil deposits that were up to three inches thick.

In the days that followed, much of the *Metula's* cargo was pumped into smaller tankers. Made lighter, the *Metula* floated again and was towed to Ponta Arenas, Chile's southernmost city. But the operation took several weeks, and by that time some 300,000 barrels of oil had entered the water.

Because the area where the *Metula* went aground was so remote, the accident never received much attention. But early the next year, another supertanker rammed into a shoal, and this time the mishap was reported in big, bold headlines almost everywhere in the world.

The ship involved was the *Showa Maru*, a 237,000-ton tanker that was carrying crude from the Persian Gulf to Japan, and which went aground at the southeastern end of the Strait of Malacca near Singapore. About 25,000 barrels of oil from the vessel's three damaged tanks seeped into the water, producing a slick ten miles long and, in some places, two inches thick.

While the size of the spill was not nearly as big as that created by the *Metula,* the impact was greater. The

500-mile Strait of Malacca passes between the Malay Peninsula and the Indonesian island of Sumatra. Both Malaysia and Indonesia had long been uneasy about the growing amount of tanker traffic using the passage, and the incident involving the *Showa Maru* served to increase the anxiety of these two nations. Apologies streamed from Japan in the days following the accident.

Two more supertanker losses occurred in 1976. One involved the 280,000-ton *Olympic Bravery,* which went aground on the French side of the English Channel. Although the vessel was—fortunately—empty of cargo, its own fuel supply fouled the beaches near the accident scene.

Every time there is a supertanker grounding, it adds to the controversy over whether these vessels should be built with double bottoms. A double bottom is just what the name implies, a second skin beneath the vessel's hull that runs the entire length of the ship. It provides an additional barrier that would have to be pierced before the oil could flow out.

Seemingly, this is an important advantage. Yet the double-bottom concept has many opponents. The American Institute of Merchant Shipping, for example, argues that double-bottom construction might be helpful in preventing oil spills in some minor groundings, but declares it has little value in the case of serious mishaps.

A double bottom could, in some cases, even add to the seriousness of a grounding. The first thing that happens when a ship's outer skin is pierced is that the space in between the two "bottoms" fills with water, and the ship loses buoyancy. Naturally, settling deeper in the water compounds the problems.

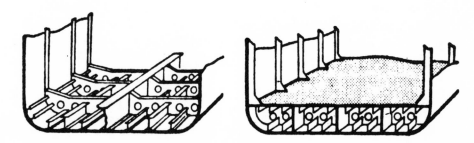

Single bottom (right) and double bottom

Another drawback to the double bottom has to do with the highly explosive vapors that can be produced by crude oil. Such gases could result from oil cargo seeping into empty double-bottom spaces, causing a hazard to the ship and its cargo, not to mention the crew.

There is also the matter of cost. One industry source says that to equip a supertanker with a double bottom would increase its cost by from 10 to 20 percent, a cost that would ultimately have to be borne by the consumer.

When the hull of a conventional tanker is split open because it runs up onto a shoal, it seldom means that its entire cargo load is going to pour into the sea. When the *Metula* went aground in the Strait of Magellan while fully loaded, the vessel was pounded on the rocks by strong currents and storms for more than a month.

About 25 percent of the ship's cargo was lost. While this could never be considered a minor spill, the reason it wasn't more serious was because the *Metula's* cargo spaces, like those of any tanker, were divided into many compartments, many tanks. Only the tanks that were ruptured leaked.

The American Institute of Merchant Shipping believes that double bottoms are an advantage only in the case of certain types of smaller tankers. These are vessels that are in coastwide service, and which are likely to carry refined petroleum of several different types. The double hull, offering as it does, a flat surface at the bottom of the cargo tanks, is easier to clean and thus makes for speedier cargo handling.

When it comes to preventing tanker groundings, collisions, and other mishaps, double bottoms are not the answer. "The *Argo Merchant* could have had a *triple* bottom," says one oil company executive, "and it wouldn't have made any difference."

A closer look at the individuals who man the ships may be in order. Industry studies show that a high percentage of tanker accidents are caused by human error. "Accidents are the direct results of people on ships," says William O. Gray, Senior Advisor of Exxon's Transportation Operations Division. "Either they do something they shouldn't have done, or they don't do something they should have done."

The 270,000-ton *Conoco Europe* holds over 2 million barrels of oil, ten times the amount carried by the *Argo Merchant*.

Human error can have any one of a number of root causes. It can result from sickness or fatigue, carelessness or negligence, or confusion or anxiety. Drunkenness can be a factor.

Accidents that result from human error can be reduced by the traffic-control procedures mentioned earlier in this chapter. More thorough training can also help.

"Without a properly trained crew," says William O. Gray, "even the best built and most meticulously maintained ships with the most sophisticated equipment are a threat."

Some shipowners aren't concerned about how their crewmen perform their shipboard duties, and maintenance means little to them. Such owners should be made answerable to international laws and maritime regulations. As it is, such laws have no teeth. They're virtually unenforceable.

The immediate future is not bright. With tanker calls on American ports constantly increasing, the number of groundings and collisions can only go higher and higher.

Supertankers can make a contribution by reducing the amount of traffic. One 270,000-ton tanker can deliver ten times as much oil as the *Argo Merchant* carried.

This shouldn't imply that supertankers in themselves are the solution to the problems now associated with importing oil. Not by any means. But they can help.

Glossary

AFT—Toward, at, or near the stern of a ship.

AMERICAN INSTITUTE OF MERCHANT SHIPPING—An organization of about 35 tanker and dry cargo ship companies which own and operate approximately one-half (300) of the oceangoing vessels in the U.S. Merchant Marine.

BALLAST—Heavy material, such as seawater, carried in a ship's tanks to increase the vessel's stability in the water.

BARREL—A unit of liquid measure equal to 42 U.S. gallons.

BEAM—The width of a ship at its widest point.

BEARING—In shipboard navigation, a direction or relative position.

BOW—The front part of a ship.

BRIDGE—The area from which the ship is navigated. It includes the wheelhouse and chart room.

BULKHEAD—An upright partition—a wall—used to divide a ship into compartments.

BUNKER—A ship's tank used for fuel oil storage.

CHARTER—To hire or lease a vessel.

CHRONOMETER—An exceptionally precise clock.

COMPARTMENT—Any subdivision of space in a ship; a room.

CRUDE OIL—Petroleum as it is pumped from the ground before it is refined.

DEAD RECKONING—A method of determining a ship's position by applying to a previously determined position the course and distance traveled since.

DEADWEIGHT TONS—The actual carrying capacity of a ship measured in long tons. Includes, besides cargo, the crew, fuel, supplies, and spare parts.

DEBALLASTING—To discharge seawater from the cargo tanks.

DRAFT—The depth of a vessel's keel below the waterline.

FATHOMETER—An instrument that reports ocean depths beneath a ship.

FIX—A ship's position as established by celestial navigation or radio.

FLUE GASES—The waste gases generated by a ship's boiler.

FORECASTLE—A raised deck near the bow of a ship.

FRAME—One of the strenthening members in a ship's hull.

GALLEY—The kitchen of a ship.

GANGWAY—The raised metal walkway that extends fore and aft on a tanker's deck.

GYROCOMPASS—A navigational compass containing a gyroscope.

HELMSMAN—A crewman assigned to steer the ship.

HOLD—A large compartment in the lower part of a ship for storing cargo.

HULL—The watertight shell of a ship.

IMCO—See Intergovernmental Maritime Consultative Organization.

INTERGOVERNMENTAL MARITIME CONSULTATIVE ORGANIZATION (IMCO)—A United Nations organization with slightly more than 100 member nations whose representatives meet periodically to establish regulations for maritime operations.

ISHERWOOD SYSTEM—Named for British shipwright Joseph Isherwood, a type of ship construction that contributed to the development of bigger tankers.

KEEL—The main fore and after structural part of a ship, usually in the form of a plate, extending from stem to stern along the center line.

KEROSENE—A thin oil derived from petroleum and used as a fuel in lamps.

KNOT—A unit of speed equal to one nautical mile per hour (about 1.15 statute miles per hour).

LIGHTER—To transfer oil cargo from a large ship to a smaller one.

LINE OF POSITION—In shipboard navigation, an imaginary line from the vessel to the point on the ocean directly below the sun, moon, or a particular star.

LOAD LINE—See Plimsoll line.

LONG TON—A ton equal to 2,240 pounds.

LORAN—A long-range navigational system based on radio signals from ground stations. Word is derived from **lo**ng **ra**nge **n**avigation.

LOT—A method of washing and loading cargo tanks in which the new crude oil is pumped in on top of the wash water at the tank bottom. Later the water is pumped out. Term is acronoym derived from **lo**ad **o**n **t**op.

MAGNETIC COMPASS—A compass that shows direction relative to the earth's magnetic field.

MARISAT—Any one of a number of communications satellites that link ships at sea with shore facilities.

MASTER—The captain of a merchant ship.

MATE—A deck officer ranking below the master.

MESSROOM—The dining room of a ship.

MONKEY ISLAND—A ship's topmost deck, usually located above the bridge.

OPEC—See Organization of Petroleum Exporting Countries.

ORGANIZATION OF PETROLEUM EXPORTING COUNTRIES (OPEC)—An organization that coordinates and unifies petroleum policies of member nations. These include Algeria, Ecuador, Gabon, Indonesia, Iran, Iraq, Kuwait, Libya, Nigeria, Qatar, Saudi Arabia, United Arab Emirates, and Venezuela.

PETROCHEMICALS—Chemicals made from crude oil.

PETROLEUM—The natural, thick, dark-colored, flammable liquid found beneath the earth's surface, used to produce fuel oil, lubricants, kerosene, asphalt, and other products.

PLIMSOLL LINE—The set of lines marked on the hull of a ship that indicate the depth to which it may be legally loaded.

POOP—A raised deck at the rear of a ship.

ROLL—Side-to-side motion of the ship.

RUDDER—A large, heavy, often rectangular-shaped plate, hinged to a rudder post, and used for steering a ship.

SEXTANT—A navigational instrument used for measuring the altitudes of celestial bodies.

SONAR—An electronic system that transmits sound waves through water and interprets the waves reflected; derived from the words **so**und **na**vigation **r**anging.

STEM—The forging or casting that forms the extreme bow portion of the ship.

STERN—The rear part of a ship.

TUN—A cask for carrying liquid; a liquid measure equal to 252 gallons.

TURBINE—An engine in which a bladed wheel is made to revolve through the force of steam produced in the ship's boiler.

ULCC—See Ultra Large Crude Carrier.

ULTRA LARGE CRUDE CARRIER (ULCC)—A tanker bigger than 350,000 tons.

VERY LARGE CRUDE CARRIER (VLCC)—A tanker between 200,000 and 350,000 tons.

VESSEL TRAFFIC SERVICE—Operated by the U.S. Coast Guard, a system of monitoring and controlling ship movements within a given harbor.

VLCC—See Very Large Crude Carrier.

VTS—See Vessel Traffic Service.

WELDING—The joining of two metal parts by fusing metal in between them.

INDEX